· WARD LOCK MASTER GARDENER ·

Patio Gardening

DAVID TOYNE

WARD LOCK

First published in Great Britain in 1993
by Ward Lock Limited, Villiers House, 41/47 Strand,
London WC2N 5JE, England
A Cassell Imprint

British Library Cataloguing in Publication Data
is available upon application to the British Library

ISBN 0-7063-7105-4

Text filmset by RGM Associates, Southport
Printed and bound in Singapore

Previous page: **A mixture of hard surfaces and foliage
provide a range of textures pleasing to the eye.**

Page 4: **Use patio plants in beds, borders, on adjacent walls
and fences; through paving, and in containers of every
type.**

Contents

Preface

The promise of more leisure time never seems to be fulfilled. In fact, in modern life we all have to run faster just to stand still and what spare time we have becomes all the more precious. It is not surprising, therefore, that relaxing at home and enjoying every available instant of good weather on our own doorstep, has become vitally important and has contributed considerably to the rise in popularity of the patio.

But, although we seem to know the value of our relaxing time, so many patios start out, and end up, as just grey slabs. It is easy to arrive at the conclusion that many of us are not making the most of our relaxing space! This book is the first step in showing you how to set about doing just that!

You do not have to be a keen gardener, although if one member of the family shows just a little enthusiasm it is almost certain to be infectious. In any case, the final effect will be to give all of you somewhere to be together while each relaxes in his or her own way – and, gardener or not, none of you will be able to deny how much the patio garden contributes to your wellbeing!

Whether remodelling an existing patio or designing a brand new one, my aim is to provide practical ideas, to give encouragement and, above all, to point out that, although it is bound to include some hard work, making a patio garden is not difficult. So I have included chapters on basic planning and design – to help you to make decisions on whether the features you would like are the most practical – information on the materials to use and even the basics of construction and maintenance for the do-it-yourself enthusiast. And, for the finished patio, suggestions on furniture, barbecues, water features, lighting, even safety – not to mention ideas from America you might like to take advantage of.

But, of course, my main purpose is to emphasize the importance and simplicity of using plants – surrounding the patio, in beds, borders and on adjacent walls and fences; through the paving, in special planting positions; and, most important of all, on the patio itself, in containers of every size and description.

The plants are so important that a special effort has been made to include extra information on the conditions they prefer, how to plant and look after them and their special needs in pots, window boxes and hanging baskets. Special varieties are recommended wherever possible, and they have all been chosen for being a little out of the ordinary, too, as well as complementing each other and their surroundings. Yet none of them are difficult to grow or difficult to buy – although one or two of the alpines may require a visit to a specialist nursery!

Finally, it is perhaps most important to point out that the ideas, suggestions, methods, materials and plants I have put together are for you to choose from – to select those you like, to reject those you do not and to mix and match as you see fit. Gardening, and particularly patio design, with its diversity of features and contrasting materials, is intensely personal. I think I have given you all the essential ingredients for success – I hope you will agree.

D.T.

ACKNOWLEDGEMENTS

The publishers are grateful to the following for granting permission to reproduce the following colour photographs: Photos Horticultural Picture Library (pp. 9, 29, 40, 44, 52, 64, 65, 88 & 92); Harry Smith Horticultural Photographic Collection (pp. 16, 17, 20, 48, 53, 89 & 93); Jerry Harpur (p. 60); A–Z Botanical Collection Ltd (p. 72); David Toyne (pp. 72 & 77); and Tania Midgley (pp. 80 & 85).

The photographs on pp. 1, 12, 13, 21, 24, 25, 32, 37, 40, 68, 69, 73, 77 & 81 were taken by Clive Nichols.

The line drawings were drawn by Vana Haggerty F.L.S. and Nils Solberg.

·1·
What is a Patio?

It is generally believed that gardening, as distinct from farming and agriculture, started in the Middle East more than four thousand years ago. So it is not really surprising that the many gardens we first hear of in Persia, were enclosed by buildings and walls for privacy, making a cool haven from the heat of the day.

The idea of the walled Persian garden was carried through Europe by the Romans, and the inner, open courtyard garden, completely surrounded by the house, has become our modern view of the typical Roman villa. The Roman courtyard was known as the *atrium*, which is now used to describe the open area in the centre of modern office buildings and shopping precincts, often enhanced with exotic plants.

Much later than the Romans, the Moors took courtyard gardens to Spain by the southern route through Egypt and north Africa; and it was the Moors who gave them the name 'patio' but, unlike the Romans, emphasized the Persian theme of water.

'Real' patios

In Granada, this can still be seen in the Alhambra, where the *Patio de los Arrayanes* (the Courtyard of Myrtles) has a long, still pool lined by clipped myrtle (*Myrtus communis*) hedges and surrounded by arched three-storey buildings. In contrast, the narrow *Patio de la Riadh* (the Courtyard of the Pool) in the Generalife Palace has a long central 'canal' with burgeoning flower borders and wall plants, and water jets playing on the surface along its whole length.

Even in Spain, however, this kind of patio is the exception, the modern version being a simple paved courtyard. This probably best describes what we now think of as a patio in the modern garden – essentially a neatly paved area more or less next to the house but now intended to be more a suntrap than a shady retreat.

Terraces

In reality, the word 'terrace', reminiscent of Victorian tea parties, is far more apt, both in origin and use. In Italian, *terrazo* means bad soil, and was used to describe the area around the house, where useless soil or rubble was dumped. This naturally tended to form a raised area and, equally naturally, became a place for sitting out, for which fertile soil is not a necessity – in other words, the modern patio!

THE MODERN PATIO

Today a patio can be just about any area with some form of hard, all-weather surface – from a small square of paving slabs to the most elaborate structure with steps, walls, raised beds, screens, pergolas and, of course, a barbecue.

Practical considerations

There are, as always, a few practical considerations which may affect what you can have and, therefore, the design. The main use of the patio comes into this category as this will determine the features and materials which are included. If it is mainly for children, gravel or pebbles will not be suitable and steps or a pool could be dangerous for little ones. For sunbathing, or in a shaded place, overhead cover will not benefit your tan or the plants growing underneath, although a covered, all-weather sitting area is a good idea.

Note the position of the services – manhole covers, water, gas and electricity pipes, and overhead wires. Most are difficult to move and some must have access.

Consider what to do about immovable objects, like buildings and trees – how to disguise or cover them for instance. Many trees and shrubs you may want to move, or even keep as part of the design.

Necessary inclusions

When you have compared what you want with what is practical, draw up a list of possibilities and add in the necessities. Paving must come first – consider size, position, material and construction. Then privacy – what will be needed to ensure seclusion and, if possible, quiet. The right screens in the right place can, for instance, cut down external noise, too.

A water supply is not absolutely essential but water is so important you really should include a tap if possible.

Style

Match the style of the patio to the house. Ultra-modern plastic and tubular steel will not blend with a thatched cottage, nor rustic poles and thatch with a modern terraced house. If for no other reason than the extra value it adds to the property, pay careful attention to blending the patio with the house.

A matched theme from indoors onto the patio is possible, especially with linked house plants and container plants outside. Quite a broad range of more practical materials will blend very successfully; the use of wood immediately comes to mind in this context.

Plants

The relationship of the patio to the rest of the garden is also important and although these can be quite different, a definite boundary – a hedge, wall, gateway or arch – will define the two areas and draw the eye through naturally. How plants are used and whether they are part of the design, or accessories added afterwards, depends on personal taste and how keen a gardener you are. However, plants offer an opportunity that almost nothing else associated with patio design can give. They can provide colour and interest, variety and change all year round, they create atmosphere and, perhaps most important, they offer something at all levels – on the ground, in the centre field, at eye level and overhead.

Location

In its original location the patio was intended to give a cool retreat, which meant that it also provided shade. The opposite is probably now more true and the position in which it gets the most sun would almost certainly be the most popular choice.

Ideally, therefore, an open, south or south-west facing aspect is best so that it gets all the sun available and you are able to take advantage of every second of sunny leisure time. This, in

▶ From the seclusion of the sitting area, containers, hanging baskets and masses of annual flowers frame the view to the garden.

combination with surrounding walls and the screens you will probably incorporate for privacy, could make the patio into a suntrap. However, at the very least, this sheltered site and aspect will be much warmer and allow you to grow more exotic ornamental plants, fruit and vegetables, than is possible in the open garden.

The most popular, logical and, usually, the most convenient place for the patio is by the house, with access from French windows or a patio door, but this is not always the ideal south or south-west facing position. There is nothing to prevent you having a patio elsewhere in the garden, where it gets more sun, or even having more than one patio, if the garden is sufficiently large. But, remember, the whole point of a patio is its clean, all-weather access and if it is not directly by the house it must

·HANDY TIP·

When planning the position of the patio remember that the sun is always at its highest point in the sky *and* it is due south (or due north in the southern hemisphere) at 12 noon every day. Don't forget to make allowances for local, summer/winter time changes, though.

be linked to it with paved walkways, or at least stepping stones, so that you do not trail muddy footmarks indoors.

Shade is not always a problem as many plants will grow quite happily in the shade cast by house wall and fences and it is quite possible to create a peaceful, green, leafy arbour where it is very pleasant to sit and look out on the sunnier parts of the garden. Don't forget that shade also moves during the day, as the sun moves across the sky, but mainly from winter to summer as it climbs higher in the sky day by day. The shade cast by a large evergreen tree, fences or the house itself, will extend much farther in winter than in summer (Fig. 1).

Size

As modern housing usually means smaller gardens, deciding on size is often not a problem as it will simply be the area available. However, if the space is very tiny, it is best to use the whole area and make it as simple as possible because fussy designs will make the patio feel even smaller than it actually is. On the other hand, a very large patio can be a little desert-like and dividing it into distinct sections, possibly with different uses in mind, using movable screens or larger plants in tubs, gives endless scope for change and innovation.

In larger gardens, size is limited only by more practical considerations like cost, obstructions,

·FLOWERING PLANTS FOR SHADE·	
Name	**Flowering time**
Astilbe (*Astilbe×arendsii*)	Mid-summer
Busy lizzie (*Impatiens ×* 'Accent')	Summer
Dwarf rhododendron (*Rhododendron yakushimanum*)	Late spring
Hardy cyclamen (*Cyclamen hederifolium*)	Autumn
Lacecap hydrangea (*Hydrangea macrophylla*)	Mid-summer–early autumn
Lenten rose (*Helleborus orientalis*)	Late winter
Lily of the valley (*Convallaria majalis*)	Late spring
Portugal laurel (*Prunus lusitanica*)	Early summer/evergreen
Primrose (*Primula vulgaris*)	Winter–spring
Primula (many species)	Spring–summer
Ramonda (*Ramonda myconii*)	Mid-spring
Spurge (*Euphorbia robbiae*)	Early summer/evergreen
Willow gentian (*Gentiana asclepiadea*)	Mid-summer
Wood anemone (*Anemone nemorosa*)	Early spring

what you want to use it for and how it fits in with other garden features. Obviously the smaller it is the more affordable it will be, and the greater possibility there is of using the very best materials and of incorporating more of the features you would like.

Shape

The house, and the standard construction materials, tend to force a more or less formal, square shape on the patio, although this is not necessarily a bad thing as it gives a continuity with the formality of the building, while at the same time providing a contrast with the garden beyond. Irregular curves and shapes help to disguise straight lines and the basic severity of the materials. However, even square paving slabs can be staggered or laid diagonally to give indented or shaped edges, and plants flopping over these further soften the transition from formal to informal (Fig. 2). Modern paving sets and pavers are often shaped or interlocking and, as such, lend themselves to more informal patterns and curves.

Using steps

If the garden is sloping any more than 30 cm (1 ft) in 30 m (100 ft) the patio site will generally need levelling. Steps will then become essential, either changing levels on the patio itself or leading from it to the rest of the garden.

However, steps serve other purposes, too, even when not absolutely essential. The transition from patio to garden is made more distinct by steps – down, giving a broader view of the garden, or up, giving a more enclosed feel. Steps from one level to another on the patio itself, can have a dramatic effect and as little as 15 cm (6 in) can make the difference between having an interesting view and losing it altogether.

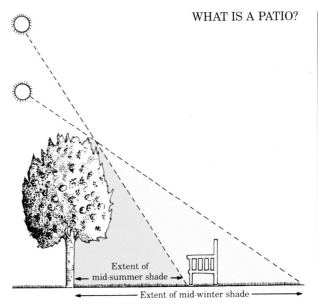

Extent of mid-summer shade

Extent of mid-winter shade

Fig. 1 Allow for greater length of shade cast by buildings and trees in winter when siting a patio, seats and plants. Early morning and late afternoon sun casts long shadows too.

Fig. 2 Even square or rectangular slabs can be softened by staggering the edges.

Inside curves

Outside edges

11

Hostas and epimediums will grow over hard stone edges to soften them.

Large patios can be divided into two, three or more small, easily managed patios. If several different levels like this are possible, don't forget that steps go up as well as down – for instance, steps up at each end and two different levels in the middle. Once again, the imagination is the only limiting factor.

Associated with a balustrade, steps add atmosphere to the outdoor room and this combination increases the tendency for the eye to be led through to the rest of the garden.

Wooden steps

When used with wooden decking, wooden steps really come into their own and they are easy to plan into the design as extensions of supporting joists and floors.

Rustic wood can be very effective, especially with older houses, or if there are trees around.

Open wooden steps over beds allow ferns and other shade plants to grow up behind them. Steps of old railway sleepers look surprisingly warm and natural, and look established and weathered the instant they are installed. Planed log poles make interesting steps, too, with short ones driven into the ground and two or three stacked behind them to form the riser. These look particularly good if they are made deeper than normal from front to back.

Slopes

Where older or less able people and small children will use the patio, bear in mind that steps may be inconvenient or unsafe. There is usually no difficulty in incorporating slopes instead of steps but an angle of 1:10, or a rise of 30 cm (1 ft) for every 3 m (10 ft) in length, is about the maximum which can be coped with, so considerably more space will be needed. All surfaces can become slippery, so ensure non-slip material, like studded paving, or treated surfaces are used.

FENCES AND SCREENS

Screens have many valuable practical uses in addition to creating privacy. Not least, they provide shelter from the wind and, especially if movable, they can put shade where it is needed. On the other hand, they also help to trap the sun. They do all this for plants as well as people – shade for ferns, sun for bedding and exotic plants, shelter for tall and tender species and support for climbers.

Screens do not have to be tall to be effective. A waist-high screen will help keep off cool winds while you eat and, made of glass, still allow you to

▶ Wooden steps leading down from the patio give a warm natural feel.

see the rest of the garden. Solid walls are impervious to light and may cause dense shade for part of the day. Soil is notoriously dry at the bottom of them, too. They are also impervious to wind which can cause gusty turbulence rather than shelter. The same is true of close-boarded fences so, in both cases, some form of perforation – gapped brick construction or open weave fencing – will break the force of the wind and still provide shelter.

Trellis can be used on walls or fences to support plants and as a screen in its own right, fixed or free-standing with feet, or even attached to a planted container. Sections can also be added to the top of solid fencing to provide a heightened but lighter screen.

·HEDGING PLANTS·		
Name	**Spacing**	**Prune***
Barberry (*Berberis*)	45 cm (18 in)	3–4
Beech	45 cm (18 in)	5–6
Box	38 cm (15 in)	4
Cherry plum	45 cm (18 in)	5
Escallonia	45 cm (18 in)	4
Euonymus	45 cm (18 in)	5
Fuchsia	30 cm (12 in)	1
Griselinia	60 cm (24 in)	4–5
Hawthorn	30 cm (12 in)	4–6
Holly	45 cm (18 in)	5
Hornbeam	60 cm (24 in)	5–6
Lavender	30 cm (12 in)	4 and 7
Lawson's cypress	45 cm (18 in)	3–4
Leyland cypress	75 cm (30 in)	7
Lonicera	30 cm (12 in)	2–7
Portugal laurel	45 cm (18 in)	3–6
Privet	38 cm (15 in)	8 or 1
Rose 'Queen Elizabeth'	45 cm (18 in)	5–6
Rosemary	38 cm (15 in)	4–5
Western hemlock (*Tsuga*)	45 cm (18 in)	4–7
Western red cedar (*Thuya*)	45 cm (18in)	4–5
Yew	45 cm (18 in)	4–5

* **KEY** 1 early spring; 2 mid-spring; 3 late spring; 4 early summer; 5 mid summer; 6 late summer; 7 early autumn; 8 mid-autumn

·HANDY TIP·

Between upright pergola supports, screens can be mounted on a central pivot so that they can be turned to give more or less shade, or shelter, depending on the weather and the plants they are protecting.

Plants as screens

Self-supporting plants make good screens, and trellis, nets or wires, will support climbers. Plants in containers, with or without supports, make movable screens.

Virtually any plants can be used, but bear in mind that deciduous shrubs, trees and climbers will allow more light through in winter and spring when it is most valuable.

● *Hedges* are special plant screens used to form a boundary and they are always planted in the open ground. Hedges usually let some wind through and therefore reduce turbulence but they cast shade and the soil at their base can be very dry, especially under privet or conifers. It is worth noting that evergreens are not always the best choice because, far from keeping their leaves on, they replace them gradually all year round and can be a nuisance, especially when near a pond or swimming pool.

Don't forget hedges need trimming, too.

MAINTENANCE

Looking after the patio really starts with your first thoughts and plans because there are a number of ways you can make it less labour intensive. For instance, large paving has less gaps in which weeds can grow and also tends to be more firmly bedded so that repairing and replacing loose pavers is less likely to be necessary. Filling the gaps with mortar will prevent weeds to a large extent but planting small alpines and ground cover plants, such as thyme, which do not object to the occasional crushing underfoot, will give a more pleasing soft and natural feel.

Careful choice of shrubs and trees will give contrast in size, shape and shades of green, gold, red and blue foliage. The idea is to do away with the annual work of planting bedding or dividing and tending perennials. Ground cover plants and planting more closely together will exclude potential weed problems, too, and aiming for an informal look, with plants flopping over edges, helps to disguise unruliness.

Weeds

Fortunately, weeds are not a great problem around the patio. They are relatively easy to dig out of the gaps in paving with an old knife, and they can also be prevented with a residual weedkiller, containing aminotriazole, to kill weeds, and simazine to stop new seeds germinating. This type of weedkiller is best as it needs only one treatment annually.

Mulching stops most weeds naturally and makes any perennial ones that come through easy to pull out. Use granite chippings on alpine beds, pebbles or cobbles around plants in planting stations or in large containers and bark chipping or one of the special plastic sheet mulches on open beds among trees, shrubs and herbaceous plants. Before mulching clear the ground with glyphosate, which is biodegradable.

General cleaning

Regular sweeping is essential and a good stiff yard broom is the best tool as it will be suitable for all surfaces, even walls and fences. Wetting the surface first will help to get off superficial marks. For more stubborn stains there are special liquid

Fig. 3 Replacing paving slabs.

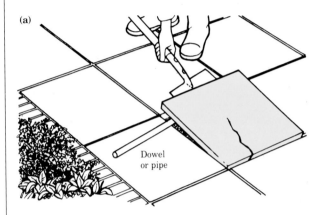

(a)

Dowel or pipe

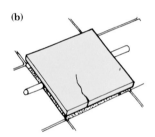

(b)

(a) Insert spade-edge down crack between paving and lever up. Use thick dowel or pipe to hold in place once lifted.

(b) Use dowel or pipe as roller to lift slab completely and roll away. Reverse procedure to put new slab in place.

cleaners which, used with the broom or a scrubbing brush, will usually take care of moss and slimy green algae which can make patio surfaces and steps, especially wooden ones, extremely slippery and dangerous. Be careful not to be too thorough though. Some paving, like bricks, setts and natural York stone, produces a lovely mellowed patina in time which adds considerably to the atmosphere and charm!

Wood preserving

All woodwork – decking, pergolas, fences, furniture, etc. – must be checked regularly for signs of decay or rot. Moss and algae can usually be scrubbed off but a sprayed-on liquid dichlorophen

Remove weeds from cracks in paving with an old knife and encourage flowers to spread.

moss killer, or a tar oil winter wash helps to make a longer lasting job.

Most timber used for garden structures is now thoroughly pressure treated with preservative and guaranteed against rot for some years, so if you prefer the weathered look that develops as the wood ages, there is no necessity to retreat every year with preservative – an invaluable attribute where fences and trellises are inextricably covered with climbing plants! However, if you would like to keep the colour and doubly insure against rot, make sure the preservative you use is safe to plants. This means not using creosote, even the fumes from which can damage plants. Of course, painted woodwork will need re-painting at least as often as external house woodwork. Use a special long-life outdoor paint. Check for flaking or blistering, scrape back to sound wood and fill, prime and undercoat before applying the new topcoat.

Metal painting

Plan to paint metal every three or four years. Scrape flaking or chipped patches back to sound paint and down to bright metal, paint with metal primer and, when dry, two top coats, or special metal paint like Hammerite.

Containers

Hosing down stone, terracotta and plastic pots *in situ* will soften dirt and algae so that it can be brushed off, but bear in mind that algae, lichen and moss are not harmful and may add considerably to the maturity of the patio scene. Watch carefully for signs of wooden containers softening, indicating rot. When wooden containers are emptied for any reason, take the opportunity to repair any damaged or rotting wood and to re-paint with a plant-safe preservative.

Hard surfaces

Unfortunately, even that most durable of paving, concrete, does not last forever. Weeding regularly will prevent any roots becoming established and widening cracks, but if cracks or edges have started to crumble they must be chiselled back to sound concrete and re-filled. Avoid frosty weather for this job.

Lifting loose paving to renew and level the base material beneath may need a spade or fork to lift the edge, and a wooden or metal pole slipped under the edge will help prevent trapped fingers (Fig. 3).

Brickwork should not need repointing any more often than elsewhere but it makes sense to check under overhanging plants or anywhere else walls are obscured.

In sheltered sites, patio paving develops a beautiful patina of moss and lichen. But take care, this can be dangerous in wet weather.

·2·
Construction

You may well have taken photographs and drawn rough sketches of how the patio might look, but it is also worth making a rough layout on site – using ropes to mark boundaries; bricks, stone or wooden planks to mark out beds and perhaps boxes to represent the main features. This will give you a much better idea of scale; to see if there is sufficient room for what you have planned.

Drawing plans
The next step is to make a detailed scale drawing of the complete patio. This will help with calculating the quantities of materials required and make it easier to include any construction details for footings, walls or woodwork, etc.

Use as large squared graph paper as is practical and, depending on the square size, choose a scale such as 3 cm to 1 m (1 in to 1 yd), or 1 cm to 1 m, if it is to be very large. This will make it much easier to relate the measurements on the plan to the actual size than the traditional 1:50 or 1:100 scale.

You will need a pencil, some paper and a clip board (pencils write on wet paper), plus a long builders' tape measure and some canes to mark the perimeter. Measure each point on the patio from two fixed points (e.g. the corners of the house) and mark the measurements on a rough plan. Make sure you measure accurately and include the position of drains and any other services or permanent objects. Transferring the measure-ments to the graph paper will give you an accurate scale plan of the site on which to draw the patio design.

Plan of action
Almost as important as the design and drawings is planning the actual work of construction or renovation:
- timing access to the site, especially if machinery or contractors are involved
- access to the house and garden
- delivery and storage of materials
- disposal of rubbish, and
- in which order it is best to do the work.

The drier months are obviously best, and earth moving and laying the paved area are a major priority, but whether walls, steps or the pergola come next depends on individual circumstances. If in doubt consult a professional garden design service as they will be able to give advice on construction in detail.

Quality and durability
When finished, the patio obviously must remain in good condition for some years without major repairs or maintenance. This means using the most substantial and durable materials possible and preparing for their installation thoroughly. For instance, using the correct type, thickness and construction for the supporting base (Fig. 4). Brick

and stone walls must have the correct depth and construction of footings for their height and thickness, and the correct mortar mix must be used. All woods must be thoroughly pressure treated, and below ground parts need to be re-treated with preservative. Posts must be set firmly in the ground to the correct depth and, if set in concrete, go through it to the soil below. Use brass or other corrosion-proof screws and fittings for all woodwork, and ensure the construction is strong enough not only to support itself but also the increasing weight of plants as they grow.

GARDEN HARDWARE

There is a vast range of materials and styles available and it will help to decide first what the patio is to be used for to determine which are impractical.

The style of the house and furnishings can influence choice if, for instance, you want to continue a theme from the living room to the patio. The shape, too, may be important – most materials lend themselves to square or angular shapes but circles and flowing curves are best constructed with smaller paving like setts or bricks. Wood is probably the most versatile of all as it blends with brick, stone and the metal associated with the house.

However the basic choice is between stone (including concrete, tiles and brick) and wood (for the paved area, steps and accessories), and metal or plastic (for accessories only).

Paving

The choice of paving is determined by taste, suitability and price. Ordinary slabs, of various colours and finishes, as well as natural stone, are the most common, economical, and therefore the most popular types available.

Fig. 4 Variations in ideal base construction for paved surfaces.

(a) Slabs.

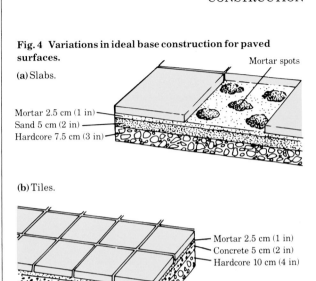

Mortar spots
Mortar 2.5 cm (1 in)
Sand 5 cm (2 in)
Hardcore 7.5 cm (3 in)

(b) Tiles.

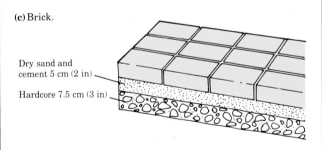

Mortar 2.5 cm (1 in)
Concrete 5 cm (2 in)
Hardcore 10 cm (4 in)

(c) Brick.

Dry sand and cement 5 cm (2 in)
Hardcore 7.5 cm (3 in)

(d) Wooden decking.

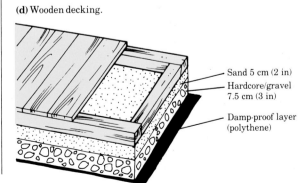

Sand 5 cm (2 in)
Hardcore/gravel 7.5 cm (3 in)
Damp-proof layer (polythene)

19

◄ Patio planters as well as construction materials should complement the style of the house.

► Pebble and cobble mulches over the soil in planting stations are attractive and easily managed.

The use of coloured dyes has increased the attractiveness of concrete but, if you do it yourself, needs a degree of skill to get a good finish.

Loose materials (gravel, cobbles, bark) are not commonly used as they do not form an even, solid base. They are, however, useful for smaller areas within the patio and especially for mulching around plants.

Real stone setts (the cobblestones of yore) have their modern imitations but both suit modern house styles very well. Tiles also fit into this category but they are generally smaller and require a cement screed on which to be laid, so the cost per square yard is relatively high.

Planting stations
It is relatively easy to leave gaps during construction, to make planting stations (Fig. 5). When paving slabs or setts are used, simply ensure any sand and cement is removed and prepare the soil in the stations as recommended on page 30, being careful not to move or damage the surrounding paving.

If the patio is constructed of concrete, spaces must be left in the base material through to the soil. Wooden edging is then used to form boxes around which the concrete is laid. Extra peat must be added to the soil as the cement surround may release lime which could adversely affect some plants.

21

Fig. 5 **Planting station construction through a solid base.**

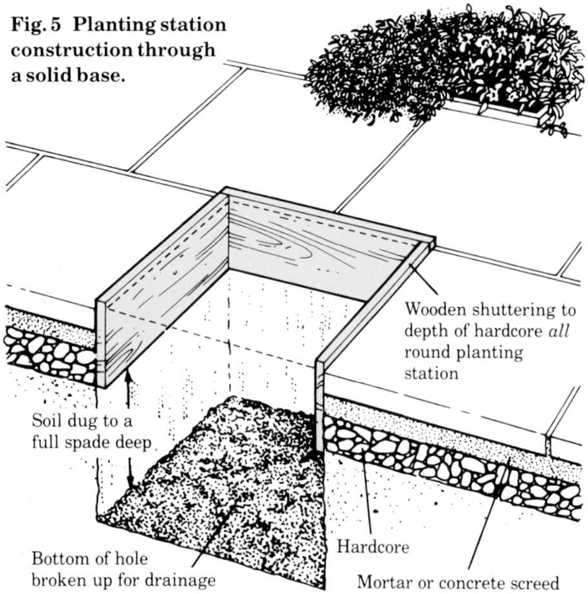
Wooden shuttering to depth of hardcore *all* round planting station
Soil dug to a full spade deep
Hardcore
Bottom of hole broken up for drainage
Mortar or concrete screed

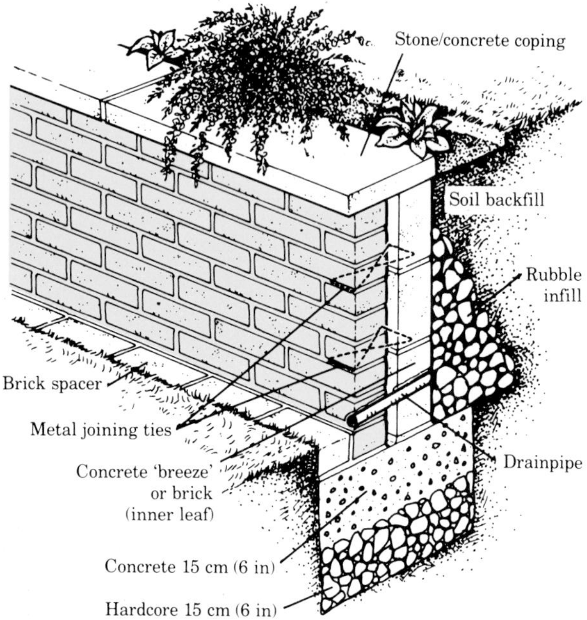
Stone/concrete coping
Soil backfill
Rubble infill
Brick spacer
Metal joining ties
Drainpipe
Concrete 'breeze' or brick (inner leaf)
Concrete 15 cm (6 in)
Hardcore 15 cm (6 in)

Fig. 6 Double/single brick wall construction. With earth infill behind, the wall must be double brick or brick/concrete block. Single brick 'above ground' walls are constructed the same without inner leaf.

·HANDY TIP·

Soil is not only heavier when it is wet, it moves more easily, too, and light sandy or gravelly soil moves most easily. It is therefore dangerous to build retaining walls more than 1 m (3 ft) high without special construction advice.

In wooden decking, planting stations are also built-in during construction and all wood must be protected from wet conditions by treating with a plant-safe preservative, at least once a year.

Walls

On a sloping site, which goes up or down more than 30 cm (1 ft) in every 30 m (100 ft), some levelling will be necessary to make a sufficiently flat paved area. A small patio on a gentle slope can be levelled by eye, and a board and spirit level used to get the final 'fall' correct. Steeper slopes will need to use the 'cut-and-fill' method and boning rods.

As a rule, a change in level of 30 cm (1 ft) on firm clay soil and 15 cm (6 in) on light or sandy soil, can be banked and grassed over but anything higher than this will need a retaining wall (Fig. 6). The absolute maximum is 1 m (3 ft) for a retaining wall too. Any higher will need more than one level, or a professional builder, as the wall must be specially designed to take the enormous weight of the soil behind it.

The first stage of levelling is to remove the topsoil and stack it away from the working area. When the levels are finished it can be returned or used elsewhere in the garden. When digging out, keep away from the house foundations and underground services. Finish the levels short of their final positions and angled backwards up the bank, to allow space to dig the wall footings. When the wall

·EVERGREEN LOW-GROWING PLANTS·	
Name	**Description**
Broom (*Cytisus×Kewensis*)	Pale yellow pea flowers
Cassiope	White flowers
Cassiope tetragona)*	
Heather (*Erica carnea*	Spreading; rich pink flowers
'Springwood Pink')*	
Hebe	Blue foliage, purple flowers
(Hebe×'Carl Teschner')	
Ling (*Calluna vulgaris*	Golden foliage, pink flowers
'Fox Hollow')*	
St Daboec's Heath	Mauve or white flowers
(*Daboecia cantabrica*)*	
Sun rose (*Helianthemum*	Double bright red flowers
nummularium 'Fireball')	
Whipcord hebe (*Hebe*	Bronze, conifer-like foliage
ochracea 'James Stirling')	
* All need acid peaty soil	

is finished, fill in with topsoil to make a bed directly behind it (Fig. 6).

Footings for a wall up to 90 cm (3 ft) high should be at least 38 cm (15 in) deep and wide, with a 15 cm (6 in) layer of concrete in the bottom. Double brick with cavity is essential as in house construction, although single brick can be built on top, above soil level. Dry stone walls need the same footings but should lean backwards into the bank for extra strength. Drainage channels must be left through the base of the wall, by inserting pieces of 5 cm (2 in) plastic drainpipe while it is being built. The best way to keep these open is to cover their inner ends with large pebbles or chippings. Higher up the wall this same technique can be used to make planting stations for wall plants and alpines.

Built-in furniture

For flexibility, it is best to plan some ordinary, movable seating and table arrangements but built-in furniture saves space and increases the feeling of spaciousness on smaller patios. It is practical, too,

as benches in particular can include storage space inside or underneath for patio accessories, tools and toys.

The main posts of a pergola will support a fixed open seat or table, or the luxury of a swinging seat (Fig. 7). Walls can be topped by a wooden bench, and a pillar or tree invites a circular wooden bench around it with loose cushions, and storage space underneath, in which they can be stored.

A sitting recess in a built-in stone or brick wall, planted with non-flowering chamomile (*Anthemis nobilis* 'Treneague') makes a scented cushion, although it can feel a little hard, not to mention damp, after sitting for a while. Seating on the retaining wall of a raised bed gives practical assistance when tending the plants, especially for elderly or less mobile gardeners.

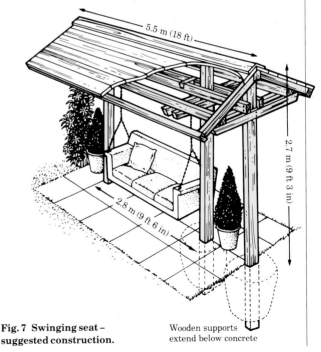

Fig. 7 Swinging seat – suggested construction.

Wooden supports extend below concrete

Just as a built-in cooker is part of the kitchen furniture, so a barbecue can be built in to the patio. The simplest construction is similar to an open-backed bench, perhaps supported by the brick piers of a wall, if they are tall enough to give a good working height. This could be used with a portable barbecue or, of course, a permanent one with built-in ash tray and griddle space too. Or be a little different with the American idea of a fire pit and surrounding built-in bench, to set the scene for camp fire sing-songs!

Wooden decking construction is easily designed to incorporate seats, benches, tables and cupboards. A main support, extended where levels change, will carry a bench seat, and broad wooden steps often make comfortable seats themselves.

Modern hardwood decking particularly lends itself to designs and features associated with water.

Wooden decking

Using wood as the main paving material (decking) has many advantages but, it has to be admitted, if any sizeable area is involved, it can be quite an expensive proposition, especially if redwood (cedar) or hardwood (such as oak or even teak) are used. Softwood (pine or spruce) decking is less expensive but, if this is your choice, make certain it is thoroughly treated with preservative and free from splinters too. Whatever wood is used, non-corroding brass fittings and screws will be necessary.

Perhaps one of the main advantages of wooden decking is that, on sloping sites, soil moving and excavation is largely unnecessary because it is supported on its own timber 'legs'. Crossing uneven ground, perhaps to join two separate patio areas with a wooden bridge, becomes quite a simple prospect, which it would not be using other materials.

The general lightness of wood comes into its own for roof gardens where too much weight can be disastrous. Decking is usually slatted to allow water to drain through, which is an added benefit for roofs, balconies and patios.

Raising wooden decking allows air to circulate beneath and through it, avoiding many problems associated with damp and stagnant conditions. Therefore, if it is to be laid on an existing paved area or on flat ground, it must be raised slightly to allow air circulation. Preservative-treated wooden blocks nailed or screwed to the underside provide a way of doing this but the surface to be covered must be stable and firm for this method, with a proper foundation if necessary. When supporting legs are used they should be set in concrete.

Mirrors

Glass mirrors, by reflecting a true image, can make a small patio, or especially a narrow one, really feel much larger and careful placing of plants, so that

An impression of
perspective and space can
be created with mirrors or
trompe l'oeil trellis arches.

reflections only occur from certain angles, heightens this effect, when obvious mirror-images can detract a little. Odd effects can be deliberately achieved by using mirrors on opposite sides to reflect each other's scenes endlessly, or by using plastic mirrors which do not give a true image but distort the view, sometimes to fairground proportions.

Mirrors are equally useful for lighting up an otherwise too dark, shady corner, and giving more planting room or allowing a favourite plant, instead of only ferns, to be grown.

Careful handling and mounting of mirrors is essential, using special rubber washers, and make sure the screws fit the holes very loosely, otherwise summer warmth may cause them to break the glass as they expand.

OVERHEAD STRUCTURES

Pergolas, walls and screens define the limits of the patio and provide privacy but overhead structures bring a much stronger feeling of a room outdoors and turn privacy to seclusion. Even an arch leading from the patio, by its association with doors and rooms, has this effect to a certain degree but once there is some form of cover directly overhead, no matter how open to the sky, there is a feeling of complete enclosure. If the structure joins directly onto the house, it will be all the more so.

There is no single name which applies to all the types of overhead structures. Free-standing ones, if more or less roofed over are called 'gazebos', but perhaps a more suitable general name, although not strictly correct in all cases, is the 'pergola'.

Fig. 8 Pergola – methods of constructing and joining beams and rafters.

(a) Beam construction and joining.

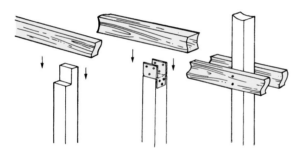

(b) Rafter connections.

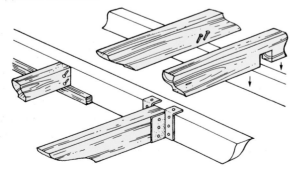

Pergolas (Fig. 8)

As well as the atmosphere it creates, and being a support for climbing plants, the pergola can provide overhead shelter from sun or rain and, because the sun cannot always be relied upon, perhaps it would be wise to consider first just how much protection from the elements you would like. The pergola certainly does not have to cover the whole patio nor, conversely, does it have to cover it *only*.

It may be that a large pergola attached to the house would make it too dark indoors, in which case a narrow covered-walk style, across the back of the house or even a central pergola separated from the house by a space open to the sky and air would be more appropriate. To take the other extreme, a pergola extended beyond the patio to make an extended arch or shade area over water or a fern bed will give an extraordinary feeling of spaciousness, and again it does not have to be connected to the house if there is a light and sunny spot that could be taken advantage of.

● *Protective cover.* Covered with climbing plants the pergola will give considerable shade but not necessarily a great deal of protection from rain. So, it may be a good idea to consider ways of providing a waterproof covering. Just as the pergola itself does not have to be defined by the size of the patio, protective covering neither has to cover it all or be permanent. Of course, if you have opted for a narrow structure attached to the house there is no reason why it should not be completely and permanently covered. In fact it is probably easier and more convenient to do it that way and, if the size has to be limited to allow light indoors, glass or clear plastic is probably the best choice. Glass can be difficult or even dangerous to handle in high places and the safer, wire-reinforced type does not look terribly attractive. There are various plastics. Single, double or triple-skinned acrylic sheet is perhaps the most common but it is more expensive than glass. Original 'perspex' is still available, but this scratches rather easily and it is rather prone to minute cracks developing. The most economical is undoubtedly the corrugated sheeting but this is also the least elegant. Coloured plastic is also available but this obviously reduces the amount of light getting through.

Arches

If a pergola is not part of the plan an arch is a lighter alternative. As well as adding the dimension of height, like a pergola an arch also makes a definite boundary inviting you on and through. Around a door, as an open porch leading into the garden, an arch frames the view of the patio, again giving it definition.

Where plants can more or less spread at will over a pergola, an arch naturally confines them, or encourages you to train and prune them more regularly. For this reason a rose arch is particularly effective.

A really light arch, creating a different dimension and atmosphere, is one of trellis. This can easily be included in a trellis screen and gives a unique, sophisticated transition between patio and garden.

Materials for overhead structures

It is tempting to think of wood as the only material for overhead structures and there are certainly many choices of hard and soft wood – plain for do-it-

·CLIMBING PLANTS·		
Name	**Description**	**Height**
Clematis (*Clematis macropetala*)	Violet blue sepals, lighter centre	3 m (10 ft)
Climbing hydrangea (*Hydrangea anomala petiolaris*)	Self clinging, soft green leaves; white flowers	12 m (40 ft)
Climbing rose (*Rosa* 'New Dawn')	Fragrant pink flowers	3 m (10 ft)
Cup-and-saucer plant (*Cobaea scandens*)	Mauve or white flowers in green 'saucer'	(3 m (10 ft)
Euonymus (*Euonymus fortunei* 'Silver Queen')	Variegated foliage	2.5 m (8 ft)
Flame nasturtium (*Tropaeolum speciosum*)	Scarlet flowers; blue fruits	3 m (10 ft)
Honeysuckle (*Lonicera sempervirens*)	Salmon-red scented flowers	3.6 m (12 ft)
Kiwi fruit (*Actinidia chinensis*)	Vigorous, heart-shaped leaves; edible fruit	9 m (30 ft)
Ornamental vine (*Vitis vinifera* 'Brandt')	Abundant small black grapes; autumn colour	6 m (20 ft)
Sweet pea (*Lathyrus odoratus* 'Lady Diana')	Pale violet, scented flowers	2.1 m (7 ft)
Virginia creeper (*Parthenocissus henryana*)	Self-clinging; bright autumn foliage	7.5 m (25 ft)
Wisteria (*Wisteria* × *formosa*)	Scented lilac flowers; felt seed pods	15 m (50 ft)

yourself experts, or pre-formed in sections or complete kits.

There are also various plastic and metal (and plastic-covered metal) systems available, usually in a green, black or white finish. These are certainly less costly and tend to make lighter looking structures than wood, although they are generally just as strong and of durable construction. Once covered in plants they are largely hidden so do not look out of place, assuming the house and patio style are right for them.

·3·
Companion Planting

Open ground beds and borders around the patio offer the most obvious permanent planting places and a strip of soil by a wall or fence provides opportunities for planting climbers and wall shrubs, but there are limits to the effects that can be achieved with this sort of edge planting.

Planting stations
In its simplest form, a special planting station on the patio surface can be a paving slab, removed from an existing patio or left out of a new one. Two or more would make an island bed for a screen of plants. Stagger the slabs left out and carry this through to a staggered edge line, with plants such as the bugle (*Ajuga reptans*) or thyme (*Thymus serpyllus*) sprawling over and softening the edges. Leave gaps in the paving by a wall, wide enough to avoid the footings and provide space for plants.

Around the base of posts or pergolas, a small planting station would suit a grapevine, a larger one could be a mixed flower border with vigorous *Wisteria sinensis* as the climber.

Gravel, pebbles, cobbles or bark mulches can be simply scraped back and replaced when planting.

Spaces in steps and decking
The corners of steps become home to aubrietas or ferns and open wooden steps make a cool, shady place beneath them, perhaps with *Clematis Jackmanii superba* climbing through them.

Raised decking makes planting pits possible, with rails or seats around them. These can be any shape to divide or define separate areas.

Grassy banks
A grassy bank planted with crocuses, primroses, cowslips and snake's head fritillaries (*Fritillaria meleagris*), makes a natural transition from patio to garden. Use a wild grass mixture of shorter-growing species, because it will have to be left uncut until mid-summer at the earliest.

Walls for planting
Dry stone walls were almost invented for planting with *Lewisia tweedyi*, in slate, granite and other non-limey stone; or unfussy aubrietas, perennial allysum (*Allysum saxatile*), houseleeks, (*Sempervivum* sp.) and sedums. Use pieces of plastic drainpipe, 4 or 5 cm (1½ or 2 in) diameter, through brick or stone mortared walls.

PLANTING PREPARATION

Preparing for planting around and on the patio is very much the same as recommended for open soil except that it probably pays to be that little bit more thorough. The conditions – often a combination of fences, walls, woodwork, paving and even overhead shade – may make life difficult for some plants if they also have to struggle in poor soil.

The moist soil behind
retaining walls make them
ideal for trailing alpines in
nooks and crannies.

It is important to prepare the planting stations in the paved area without the compaction which is vital everywhere else for a firm level surface. Dig out planting positions as deeply as possible – 60 cm (2 ft) is best – putting the soil on a polythene sheet to keep the patio paving clean. No matter what type the soil is, thoroughly mix in composted bark or other organic conditioner, and a slow-release or organic-based fertilizer. Before refilling the planting hole, make sure the bottom is well broken up so that water can drain away freely (Fig. 9).

If a climbing frame, trellis or stake is necessary for the plant, put it in position at this stage, then return enough of the soil mixture to leave the hole the correct depth for the root ball of the plant.

In borders and beds around the patio, again dig as deeply as possible, taking care to keep away from the foundations of any walls or the supporting base of the patio paving. Incorporate the organic soil conditioner and fertilizer as before and break up the bottom of the trench with a fork. Incidentally, this is particularly important in new homes, especially where topsoil has been removed or heavy construction machinery used.

When finished, beds and borders tend to be a little higher than when started. This will settle with time but any spare can be used to level other parts of the garden.

Watering

Plants around the patio will need more water than those in the shade or open ground, particularly close to walls and fences where the soil is always drier. Plants in the paving are not quite so likely to suffer because the paving acts as a mulch but, in all cases, prepare the planting soil thoroughly as recommended above.

On a small scale, watering plants using a watering-can may be adequate but a hosepipe is

Fig. 9 Double-digging border soil.

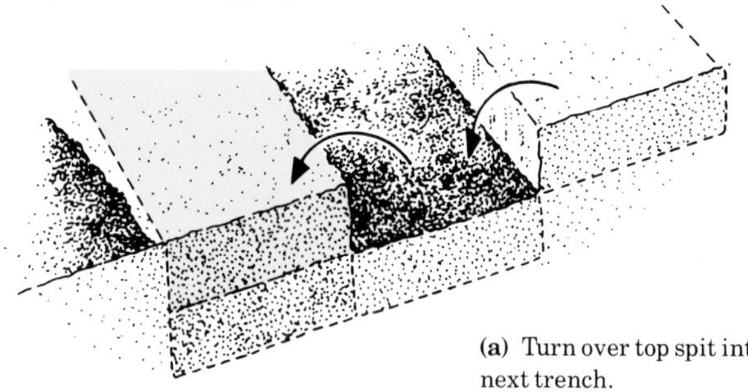

(a) Turn over top spit into next trench.

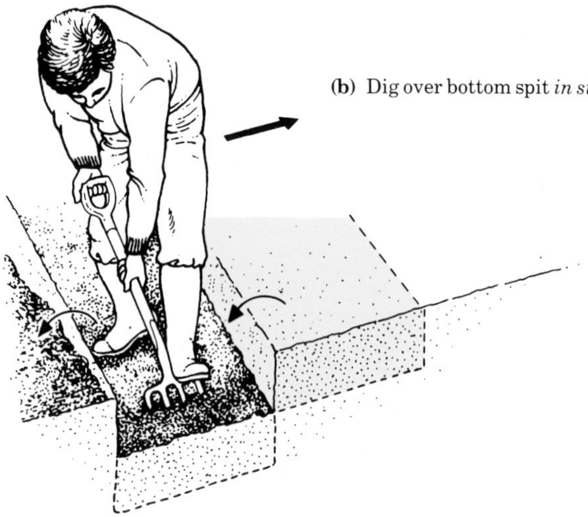

(b) Dig over bottom spit *in situ*.

(c) Planting after double digging.

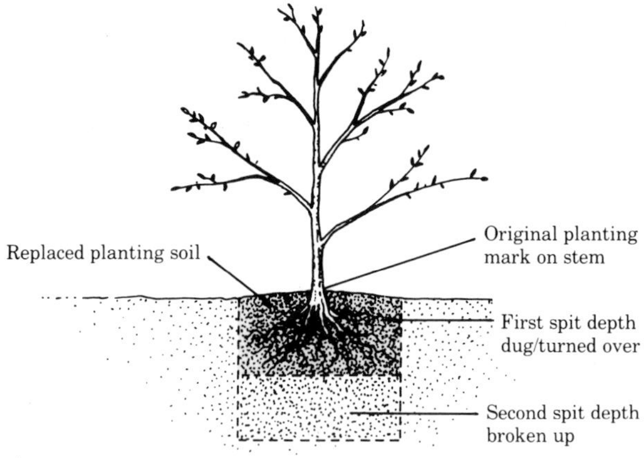

Replaced planting soil

Original planting mark on stem

First spit depth dug/turned over

Second spit depth broken up

much more convenient, and is also useful for washing down the patio, for spraying plants in dry weather and for feeding them using one of the modern hose-end dilutors.

Automatic watering systems can be hidden behind supports and under paving, and then individual nozzles will water the plants at the turn of a tap (Fig. 10).

Feeding

Preparing the planting soil with a slow release or organic-based fertilizer, as mentioned previously, will provide sufficient food for perennials, trees and shrubs in their first year. But if growth is slow, give these plants a light liquid feed using one of the concentrated soluble plant foods. In following years you can feed with a dry granular fertilizer, or an organic one like blood, fish and bone, in spring, and an occasional liquid feed later during summer.

Bedding plants are best fed weekly through the summer with a soluble plant food.

Pests and diseases

The sheltered, warm conditions on the patio can encourage pests and some fungus diseases, but the convenience of walking around it will allow you to spot problems and keep them under control easily.

Aphids (greenfly and blackfly), whitefly and perhaps red spider mite, will be the most common pests although slugs can be a problem in wet or humid weather. A general garden insecticide based on malathion will take care of all these and most others without leaving any long-lasting residues; or, if you prefer, use natural ingredients such as pyrethrum or derris. Metaldehyde slug baits come in three forms, pellets, water-on-liquid or tape for encircling plants.

Fungus diseases, on the other hand, are best prevented, as they cannot be cured once they have arrived. A good general fungicide, such as benomyl will deal with mildew and black spot, and one containing myclobutanil will also stop rust.

Plant supports

Many plants need extra support to stop them flopping over or being knocked about by the wind. Some, like the ivy *Hedera helix* 'Jubilee', have no trouble attaching themselves to walls and weathered fences and need no more than leaning in the right direction. Other self-adhesive climbers, like Virginia creeper (especially *Parthenocissus henryana*) need quite a bit of encouragement to grip the wall and will need the assistance of lead-headed nails, with a tongue to bend around the stems.

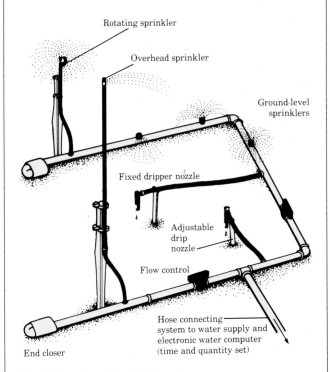

Rotating sprinkler

Overhead sprinkler

Ground-level sprinklers

Fixed dripper nozzle

Adjustable drip nozzle

Flow control

Hose connecting system to water supply and electronic water computer (time and quantity set)

End closer

Fig. 10 An automatic watering system.

Tendril climbers like clematis will be happy on a trellis or directed up canes and will require soft string or plastic covered wire, fixed so it does not pinch the stems.

Temporary supports, such as pea and bean netting are ideal for green peas and sweet peas – as well as morning glories (*Ipomoea*), black-eyed Susan (*Thunbergia alata*), and nasturtium (*Tropa-*

Roses grown over a pergola or arch create cool shady walks.

eolum majus). Twiggy pea-sticks, pushed into the soil, support bedding which tends to spread, like *Clarkia* and dwarf sweet peas.

Trees and shrubs grown with a clear trunk will need staking until they are established.

Training

Vines and trained fruit trees are simplest to deal with if some kind of framework is provided. This could be in the form of wires stretched across at 45–60 cm (18–24 in) intervals using 'vine eyes', which have a hole in their heads through which the wire passes. This method is also quite useful for roses which will need tying up like the fruit, and wisteria, which should support itself by twisting its stems around the wires as a grape vine does with its tendrils. Once clothed with branches, foliage, flowers and fruit, the wire framework does not look out of place.

Pruning

It is simply not possible to give detailed instructions on how to prune all the shrubs, trees and climbers that can be grown around the patio. But there are basic rules to pruning which should always be followed:

1. Cut out the four D's – any dead, dying, diseased and damaged shoots and branches.

2. Cut out any weak or crossing branches, to let in light and air.

3. Encourage flowers and fruit by cutting out shoots that have already flowered.

4. Prune to keep the plant to a manageable size.

5. Always use sharp tools – pruning knife, secateurs, loppers (for heavier branches) or even a pruning saw – and always cut back branches cleanly to the main stem from which they are growing, to avoid letting in disease.

6. Always prune side shoots just above a leaf scar, which is where the next shoot will grow from. Leaf scars or buds facing outwards are best.

7. Different plants need pruning at different times of the year. Check before beginning.

Winter care

Pergolas and arches, especially if they have climbing plants on them, can keep quite a few degrees of frost off plants below them. Dubiously hardy bulbs, like *Amaryllis belladonna*, and herbaceous plants like *Lobelia cardinalis*, can be saved by a heavy mulch of garden compost, peat, bark or dried leaves like bracken. Deciduous shrubs and trees, including fruit, and all exposed wooden fences, screen posts and supports can be sprayed with a tar oil winter wash, covering stone and other surfaces to prevent staining. This works wonders in reducing next year's pests, which often hibernate or leave eggs and pupae in such places.

PATIO PLANTS

Climbers

● *The hardy evergreen climbers* are limited to ivies, although there are a large number of species and varieties to choose from. The very large-leaved *Hedera colchica* 'Dentata Variegata', the red stems and gold-splashed leaves of *H. helix* 'Jubilee', the silver-white variegation of *H.h.* 'Chicago', the crimped, almost circular leaves of *H.h.* 'Cristata' and, in the sun, butter-yellow *H.h.* 'Buttercup', to name but a few.

● *The hardy flowering climbers* are all deciduous, except perhaps *Clematis armandii*. If your patio is really sheltered or has overhead protection, the exotic *Lapageria rosea* will give a genuine Mediterranean feel or, if not, try the Japanese wisteria (*Wisteria floribunda*) for a similar, but less tropical feel. Clematis are deservedly popular, especially large-flowered hybrids, but species such as *Clematis macropetala* or *Clematis montana*, will romp away vigorously in spring, with blue and white or pink flowers, respectively.

Fig. 11 Methods of attaching trellis to walls.

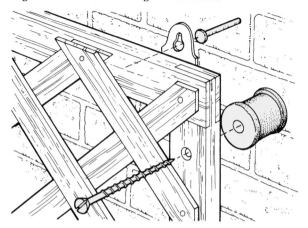

(a) Keyhole hangers or spacers.

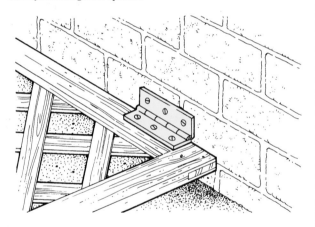

(b) A good idea – hinge trellis to make wall maintenance easier.

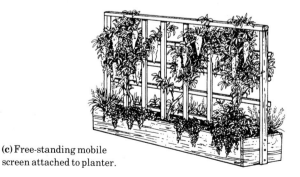

(c) Free-standing mobile screen attached to planter.

Wall shrubs

Some plants need a little help to climb (Fig. 11). The Californian lilac, *Ceanothus thyrsifolius*, has blue flowers – try the more compact varieties like 'Edinburgh' and 'Autumnal Blue'. *Euonymus fortunei* 'Silver Queen' makes a quite stunning wall of silver-white. *Cotoneaster × watererii* 'Cornubia' will produce a marvellous crop of startling red berries and even some autumn golds and oranges among its evergreen leaves. Pyracanthas too, produce white flowers in spring and a mass of red, orange or yellow berries in autumn – and they are evergreen too.

Ground cover

Ground-covering plants are valuable for smothering weeds but they can also sprawl over paving, low walls and balustrades, as well as provide colour. The periwinkle, *Vinca minor* 'Burgundy', with red flowers, makes a change from the common blue one and the variety 'Variegata' has cream-splashed leaves. Bugle, *Ajuga reptans*, is evergreen like the periwinkle; the variety 'Multi-colour' has red, gold and bronze-splashed leaves. For a large area *Rubus tricolour*, with sculptured, red-veined leaves and red hairy stems, may still need curbing from time to time. Many of the so-called alpines and border plants, particularly herbaceous geraniums, hostas and lady's mantle (*Alchemilla mollis*), are excellent summer ground cover too.

Other shrubs

The first shrub to come to mind is the Camellia. Whether it is *Camellia japonica* or the earlier flowering *Camellia × williamsii*, they both have the glory of their flowers and glossy green leaves at an easily tended height and make superb background shrubs. The Mexican orange blossom (*Choisya ternata*) has softer green three-lobed leaves which in the slower growing variety 'Sundance' are butter yellow in the sun or lime

green in the shade. Its white flowers are a little sporadic but orange blossom scented as its name suggests.

A bamboo, *Arundinaria viridistriata*, with golden yellow striped leaves on purplish bamboo canes, makes an excellent 1.5 m (5 ft) summer and winter screen. Cut down in early spring, it is much more colourful and vigorous.

Other perennials

Bearing in mind that you may not wish to obscure the view totally, it is possible that delphiniums, plume poppy (*Macleaya cordata*), and perhaps *Inula racemosa*, or even foxgloves, (*Digitalis purpurea* 'Excelsior' hybrids), may need relegating to framing positions or side borders. However that still leaves a dazzling array of medium to small plants: bleeding hearts (*Dicentra spectabilis*), *Astrantia maxima*, astilbes such as 'Fanal' or 'Hyacinth', *Lysimachia clethroides*, the evergreen *Euphorbia characias wulfenii*, *Osteospermum jucundum*, *Alstroemeria* Ligtu hybrids and *Anchusa azurea* 'Loddon Royalist'.

Spring can be a little difficult for perennial beds but the drumstick primula (*Primula denticulata*) and the candelabra primula (*P. bulleyana*), will make up for a lot in a moist border.

In autumn, elephant's ears (*Bergenia cordifolia*) turn red, and hardy red and gold chrysanthemums, pink and blue Michaelmas daisies (*Aster amellus*), and Japanese anemones (*Anemone hupehensis*) all flower. Even winter produces Christmas roses (*Helleborus niger*) and a little later the Lenten rose (*Helleborus orientalis*).

Temporary colour

Annual flowers and bedding plants can provide colour, interest and change all the year round. Hardy annuals can be sown outdoors in the autumn or spring, or in trays; half-hardy ones are limited to

· GROUND-COVER PLANTS ·

Name	Description
Barrenwort (*Epimedium macranthum* 'Rose Queen')	Variably evergreen; deep pink flowers; leaf colour
Checkerberry (*Gaultheria procumbens*)	Evergreen; dense glossy leaves; red edible berries
Common thyme (*Thymus serpyllum*)	Evergreen; tiny scented leaves; crimson flowers
Creeping Jenny (*Lysimachia nummularia* 'Aurea')	Variably evergreen; golden leaves and flowers
Houttuynia (*Houttuynia cordata* 'Chameleon')	Herbaceous; red, yellow and green leaves
Irish ivy (*Hedera helix* 'Hibernica')	Evergreen; vigorous, large leaves
Knotweed (*Polygonum affine* 'Donald Lowndes')	Deciduous; pink flowers; autumn colour
Lady's mantle (*Alchemilla mollis*)	Herbaceous; lime-yellow flowers; felted leaves
Ornamental blackberry (*Rubus tricolor*)	Evergreen; red-veined leaves, hairy stems
Pachysandra (*Pachysandra terminalis* 'Variegata')	Evergreen; variegated green leaves
Prostrate cotoneaster (*Cotoneaster dammeri*)	Variably evergreen foliage; berries; autumn colour
Prostrate juniper (*Juniperus horizontalis* 'Douglasii')	Evergreen; grey aromatic 'conifer' foliage
Waldsteinia (*Waldsteinia ternata*)	Evergreen; yellow strawberry flowers

35

indoors. Taking cuttings of perennials like pelargoniums, busy lizzy (impatiens), *Salvia farinacea* 'Victoria', *Begonia semperflorens*, and keeping them ticking over through the winter on a window sill or in a greenhouse, is a worthwhile money saver. A bed devoted to true hardy annuals, raised from seed, usually takes on a very light, airy look and is particularly good where the patio itself is light, with few dark shrubs or trees and climbers. The half-hardy annuals are heavier and some, such as zinnias and sunflowers, need to be used carefully, because they *are* so different. But, together with other bright bedding, such as *Salvia splendens* 'Lady in Red' and the strong-coloured 'Accent' strain of busy lizzies, they can give a real hot, summery feel that almost dares the weather to be anything other than sunny!

Some half-hardy bedding really worth trying are the white annual mallow, *Lavatera trimestris* 'Mont Blanc' or pink 'Silver Cup', *Salpiglossis sinuata* 'Splash' and *Convolvulus tricolour* 'Blue Flash'. Poor man's orchid *Schizanthus* 'Hit Parade' is marvellous in a sheltered, sunny spot.

Summer bedding plants are also largely annuals raised from seed, like African marigolds (tagetes) and petunias, but bedding plants also include tender and half-hardy perennials like pelargoniums, tuberous begonias and the castor oil plant, *Ricinus communis* 'Impala'.

Whichever type of annuals or bedding you grow, don't forget to take off the dead flowers and feed with a soluble high-potash feed, regularly, to get the best from them.

Alpines

The name 'alpine' originally referred to plants which are native to the world's mountain ranges and, as many are small, this has led to many other small plants which will grow happily in similar conditions being considered alpines too. But the fact is not all true alpines are small. Look out for *Dodecatheon hendersonii*, the 30 cm (12 in) high aptly named 'shooting star', with delicate cyclamen flowers on tall straight stems; *Pulsatilla halleri*, the intensely downy 20 cm (8 in) relative of the taller Pasque flower, *Pulsatilla vulgaris*, both with mauve anemone flowers. Even larger, the alpine columbine *Aquilegia alpina* reaches 45 cm (18 in) with its blue spurred flowers. For acid, peaty soil *Andromeda polyfolia* 'Alba', an open evergreen with white heather flowers and a giant again at 45 cm (18 in). Dwarf willows, *Salix hastata*, with felted leaves and silver catkins, *Salix reticulata*, with net-veined leaves and reddish brown catkins.

The dwarf alpines include such beauties as the spring gentian (*Gentiana verna*) just 5 cm (2 in) high and there are literally hundreds of tiny, mound-forming saxifrages, like *Saxifraga scardica* just 2.5 cm (1 in) high (until it flowers) and 8 cm (3 in) wide, or the lime-encrusted *Saxifraga stribovyi* with deep maroon tipped-over flowers.

The list of alpines and similar dwarf plants which like the same conditions, is endless and will make selection very difficult indeed.

Plants for paving

Most alpines can be grown in the cracks or gaps left in paving but since they may be stepped on, it's worth considering a few more resilient types which are available for this purpose. All the dwarf *Phlox* – *P. amoena*, *P. douglasii* and *P. subulata*, are suitable and spread quite well, carrying their purple, pink or white flowers in summer, although the foliage can look a little tired before autumn arrives. Succulent sedums, particularly *Sedum spathulifolium*, seem to fit the bill exactly, as does the houseleek, *Sempervivum tectorum*, looking distinctly desert-like. Thyme (*Thymus serpyllus* or *T. vulgaris*) invites a quick press of the foot to give off its scent and adds mauve or pinky flowers and

A mixed shrub and perennial border acting as the perfect foil to the patio.

many coloured-leaved varieties to its attributes. *Acaena microphylla* and *A. caesiiglauca*, from New Zealand, both have brown-red burs and creep very well.

Bulbs

The very word bulb seems to suggest spring, yet bulbs and similar plants are actually in flower every month of the year.

The very early spring bulbs like aconites and snowdrops look good in the front of any border. The first real patio bulbs however are the dwarf irises, *Iris reticulata*, *I. histrioides* and *I. danfordiae* – purple, blue and yellow respectively and looking equally natural in alpine or raised beds.

Daffodils are the next, the alpine meadow types *Narcissus bulbocodium* and *N. cyclamineus*, then their hybrids 'February Gold', 'Peeping Tom', and 'Thalia' or the larger-flowered white 'Mount Hood' and the numerous yellow varieties.

Tulips, especially the dwarf Greigii hybrids like 'Red Riding Hood', give a foretaste of summer.

Then lilies, with their beautiful forms, colours and scents, from the startling orange of 'Enchantment' in early summer to the exotic orchid pink of *Lilium speciosum* in early autumn.

Autumn brings more crocuses, the crocus-like *Colchicum speciosum* and *Nerine bowdenii*, both known as 'naked ladies', as they flower before their leaves appear.

37

·4·
Gardening with Containers

The larger the patio the more likely it is to have flat, open areas which lack interest or at least are more difficult to make attractive and inviting. Permanent planting plots around the patio can only do so much to enhance the view from the window or make sitting out a pleasant relaxation. But, although they give definition to the patio, these beds are just as likely to emphasize the emptiness and unchanging quality of the paved area. There are changes to the scene of course. Perennials, shrubs and trees putting on their seasonal shows; spring, summer and winter bedding, bulbs and annuals are all valuable in the permanent beds, but what they obviously lack is movement and surprise.

Pot pourri

There is so much space on a patio, no matter how small it may be, that it really is a crime not to invest in a movable feast of colour and variety, as well as the stationary one, by using containers to make an ever changing landscape.

Space even on the smallest patio? Of course. Containers do not only sit on the ground. Hay racks, special pots and pot hangers, and hanging baskets on brackets, can all take advantage of walls and fences. Troughs or boxes can even be fixed on top of low ones.

Hanging baskets can be used on pergolas and other woodwork or pillars, under porches, and pots or half baskets attached to uprights, too. A different approach is to use the plaited rope Japanese art of *macramé* with one, two, three, or more, ceramic or terracotta pots.

Rails and balustrades make ideal places for window boxes, one-sided or on 'saddles' to use both sides, and of course window boxes can go on the inside window sill as well as the outside. An adjacent flat roof such as a garage, if it is strong enough and has safe, easy access, can also be furnished with containers of trailing plants.

The possibilities for decoration are almost endless and, as a bonus, by making a mobile screen, containers also provide a handy way to disguise a bed of fading flowers or a temporary eyesore like builder's materials. A group of pots will even cover a manhole and leave it easily accessible.

TYPES OF CONTAINERS (Fig. 12)

Pots

Ordinary plant pots offer the greatest range of sizes and, as well as smooth, brick-red terracotta, they come decorated with various classical and modern patterns in a host of other materials and colours. Plastic is the most common and terracotta still the most popular colour. A good choice, as plastic is clean, durable, economical and there are even matt-textured pots, which are almost indistinguishable from real terracotta.

Urns and jars

Made of terracotta, stone or glazed earthenware, and the inevitable plastic, the rounded shape of the traditional urn creates a distinctive focal point. At the large end of the scale are the 'Ali Baba' jars.

Chinese ceramic urns cover the whole range of sizes, ending even larger than Ali Baba jars. They are certainly beautiful containers, if among the most expensive.

Troughs and sinks

Ceramic or stone troughs and sinks are sadly a rarity and therefore likely to be expensive. However, there are many modern versions in re-constituted stone or look-alike cement, as well as plastic and, very realistic, lightweight glass fibre.

Fig. 12 Some examples of the containers available.

Tubs and boxes

Once upon a time boxes and tubs were always wood, plastic, glass-fibre, stone and concrete are now equally common.

Tubs and boxes are generally wider then they are high, while troughs and sinks are generally shallower – that is the difference.

Growing bags

As well as for tomatoes and other vegetables, growing bags can be used to grow wonderful massed displays of bedding plants. To make them more attractive they can be encased in a special box, although well fed annuals and bedding will soon hide the bag anyway.

Hanging baskets See Chapter 7.

Window boxes See Chapter 8.

ALTERNATIVE CONTAINERS

Many throwaway plastic buckets, tubs, barrels, wooden and plastic boxes and painted metal tins, make ready-to-use containers. But there are other ways of making your own.

Constructing your own

The simplest of all is an open-bottomed container constructed of, perhaps, railway sleepers (or pieces

39

◄ Aubergines and African marigolds are a companion planting designed to discourage pests.

▼ Pots of all types are a valuable, movable asset on the patio.

of sleepers, for a planter less than 2.5m/8ft square) Less prettily, old tyres can do the same job in a different style and they are easier to handle and stack to a greater height. Wooden boxes and trough-style planters are reasonably easy to make and a source of old wood suitable for these is often available from a demolition site. The wood is best joined together with brass screws or, at the very least, galvanized nails and it must be treated with a preservative, or primed and painted, a month before it is filled and planted.

Sinks make excellent containers – old glazed earthenware kitchen sinks need quite a bit of modification so they really come under the banner of do-it-yourself, or you can make a replica completely from scratch. In both cases, this needs a special lightweight cement mixture, which simulates stone, called hypertufa. The mix is 2 parts peat, 1½ parts sand and 1 part cement, plus enough water to make it 'mouldable' but not wet or runny. Score and/or chip the outside of the glazed sink to provide a 'key' for an epoxy impact adhesive, which is spread all over the outside and 10cm (4in) down the inside. Spread the hypertufa mixture by hand on the glued surfaces, about 1cm (½in) thick, or a little more if possible, leaving a fairly rough, stone-like surface. Now you need to be patient, for you will have to keep it cool and dry for at least a month before filling.

Two large, heavy-duty cardboard boxes, one 10–13cm (4–5in) shorter, narrower and shallower than the other, are needed to make a sink from scratch. Put an 8cm (3in) layer of hypertufa in the bottom of the larger box and set four 8cm (3in) pieces of 2.5cm (1in) dowel in it. These will support the inner box and can be knocked out later to form drainage holes. The smaller box then sits inside the larger and the gap between filled with more hypertufa mixture. Battens from wall to wall inside the smaller box will stop it 'bellying'.

Standing the box in a corner with wooden boards pressed to the other two faces will also prevent the outside deforming. This, too, will need at least a month to set properly but the cardboard boxes can usually be safely removed after about 10 days. Handle the sink very carefully until it is fully hardened.

GENERAL RULES

Good looks
Large containers are usually more effective but they also dry out less quickly, which means less work watering. Smaller ones can be grouped together, with the best in front if some are less elegant than others. Small pots can also be grouped inside larger containers, plunged (buried up to their rims) in peat or expanded clay granules like Hortag.

Weight
Don't forget that, filled, planted and watered, large containers will weigh a considerable amount, so reconsider if they are to be used on a flat roof, balcony, or wall – plastic pots and soil-less compost weigh less. For the same weighty reason, always put larger containers in position before filling and planting.

The right size
Although a perennial tree or shrub may eventually grow very large, it is a mistake to plant it in too large a pot as its roots will be surrounded by empty, moist compost – a stagnant breeding ground for disease. Too small is just as bad, the roots will soon run out of space, water and food and the plant could become stunted or woody, thereby forced into premature old age.

The general rule for potting-on is to choose 'the next size up', with about 2.5cm (1in) of new compost around the root ball.

Drainage holes

Before filling with compost and planting, check all containers have clear drainage holes. Cover them with mesh – nylon, plastic or galvanized metal gauze are all suitable – to keep out unwelcome visitors such as soil pests, woodlice, slugs, even worms.

A layer of broken flower pot pieces, 'crocks', comes next, or again Hortag expanded clay granules; and if the plant is a long-term perennial, it would be a good idea to add a piece of turf, grass side down, to make an organic, water retentive layer. If turf is not available, coarse peat will serve the same purpose (Fig. 13).

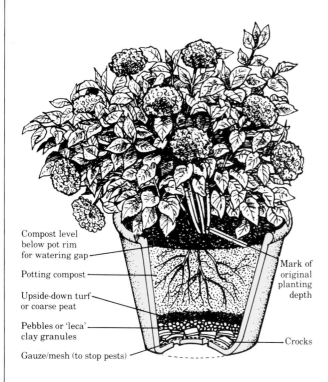

Compost level below pot rim for watering gap

Potting compost

Upside-down turf or coarse peat

Pebbles or 'leca' clay granules

Gauze/mesh (to stop pests)

Mark of original planting depth

Crocks

Fig. 13 Pot up all container-grown plants in this way.

Raising pots

To aid drainage, containers are best raised off the ground, which also deters woodlice and slugs from hiding underneath. Wooden battens are one method but must be treated with a suitable preservative because of the very wet conditions they could have to endure. There are special terracotta and stone-coloured 'feet' for this job, which enhance the look of the pots at the same time. For some other practical raising ideas see 'Moving and handling containers' on page 43.

Compost

Do not use garden soil. Specially made composts are free of pests, diseases and weeds, and they are available in different types for different plants, so that lime-loving and acid-loving plants can be grown side-by-side if you wish. For very long-term plants such as shrubs and trees, it is best to invest in a soil-based compost such as the John Innes potting composts. Replenish the nutrients by annual feeding with a long-term controlled release fertilizer, and the essential organic content by dressing annually with a soil-less potting compost or true-and-shrub mixture.

Planting ways

Always water plants well, at least an hour before transplanting, even if there is no possibility of disturbing the roots.

Soil-less composts need fairly gentle handling and should be firmed with the fingers only. Soil or loam-based composts need firmer treatment, even to ramming-in around permanent trees and shrubs.

Put a layer of compost over the crocks and lightly firm this, before adding more. The idea is to have enough compost under the plant to bring its compost surface (the mark on its stem where the original soil level was) up to about 1cm ($\frac{1}{2}$in) below the new container rim, leaving space to water.

Water the newly potted plant thoroughly, leave for a while and water it again, until a little water drains from the bottom. This shows that all the compost is evenly wetted *and* that the drainage is working.

For the first few days after potting, keep the plant shaded from sun and wind while it settles in and starts growing again.

Potting-on and transplanting

The general rule is to pot-on into the next sized pot before the plant has completely filled its old pot with roots. For many plants in small pots this will be every year and for quick-growing annuals or vegetables it could be twice or more times in a single season. Knocking the plant out of the pot is the simplest way to see how pot-bound it is. In containers with several plants this may not be quite as easy and other signs of unhappiness, such as poor growth, or easily wilting in hot weather, may have to be the guide. Transplanting is then the best course of action.

Moving and handling containers

● *Little* . . . Moving smaller, free-standing containers to give changing effects and displays is part of the fun of patio gardening. It presents no particular problems except that it is probably best done when the plants are being changed too, as existing ones may not be as happy in their new position. Some, like camellias or fuchsias, may show their displeasure by dropping their flowers before they open.

● *. . . and Large* The weight of a large tub or trough, filled with compost and plants and freshly watered, is considerable. It has already been mentioned where safety is concerned and, when it comes to moving such a container, consider your health too. Large containers are best moved as little as possible for this reason, and because it is all too easy to damage the valuable plants in them.

·ALPINES FOR SINK GARDENS·	
Name	**Description**
Alpine buttercup (*Ranunculus alpestris*)	Perennial; toothed leaves; white saucer flowers
Alpine geranium (*Geranium argenteum*)	Perennial; pink flowers; silvery cleft leaves
Alpine phlox (*Phlox douglasii*)	Perennial; pink flowers
Alpine pink (*Dianthus alpinus*)	Perennial; rose crimson flowers; narrow leaves
Cobweb houseleek (*Sempervivum arachnoideum*)	Succulent; multiple rosettes covered with white hairs
Coral bush (*Helichrysum coralloides*)	Perennial; upright, grey scale-like leaves
Meadow rue (*Thalictrum klusianum*)	Perennial; ferny leaves; tiny purple flowers
Mossy saxifrage (*Saxifraga moschata* 'Cloth of Gold')	Perennial; soft, golden, cleft leaves
Noah's Ark (*Juniperus communis* 'Compressa')	Conifer; slow-growing upright evergreen
Saxifrage (*Saxifraga cochlearis*)	Perennial; silvery pads of hard rosettes
Sea pink (*Armeria maritima*)	Perennial; evergreen grassy leaves; pink flowers
Soldanella (*Soldanella alpina*)	Perennial; leathery leaves; pink-fringed flowers
Stonecrop (*Sedum spathulifolium* 'Capa Blanca')	Succulent; small tight waxy-white rosettes

If larger containers have to be moved, wait until they are ready for watering, as drier compost is lighter. The best plan is to make them mobile before planting. Castors or wheels can be fitted to the bottom of wooden containers and pieces of dowel or galvanized water pipe – 1–4cm ($\frac{1}{2}$–$1\frac{1}{2}$in) in diameter depending on the size of the container – will act as rollers, making moving them short distances and cleaning under them much easier. Keep an extra piece of dowel or pipe to replace the back one as the container is rolled forward. Rollers also raise the container off the ground, deterring creepy crawlies and ensuring free drainage.

Growing bags are difficult to move because they are flexible, but a board underneath will make it easier. On flat surfaces a piece of plastic sheeting underneath will allow the bag to be dragged without too much trouble to another position.

WATERING

If there is one single aspect of growing plants in containers that is more important than any other, it is watering and, on a patio, where conditions are likely to be warmer and drier than the rest of the garden, it is doubly so.

Unless a torrential downpour thoroughly wets the compost, it is best to forget about rain doing the watering for you but, if the drainage has been attended to, it will be difficult to overwater in summer. So, if in doubt, or if you are away for more than a day, water–water–water!

A simple daily check to see whether the plants have enough water is to push a finger well into the compost or soil and, if it feels moist at the tip, they will be alright – until the next day at least.

Growing in a container, no matter how large it may be, plants have a limited store of water and food, and they will run out of both far more quickly than in open soil.

There are several ways of ensuring plants do not starve and using the right soil or compost is the starting point. For instance, bedding plant compost is simply not substantial enough for camellias or rhododendrons but, on the other hand, a shrub compost would be rather wasted on bedding plants. For bedding, vegetables, tomatoes or strawberries use ready-made soil-less composts or, for convenience, growing bags. For perennials, more substantial soil-based composts are best.

Fertilizer

Incorporating a long-lasting controlled-release fertilizer, when planting up, is especially useful for hanging baskets but can equally well be used for any plants. Because of the limited compost and the generally warmer conditions, it is best to use a weekly soluble or liquid feed, too, because even controlled-release fertilizers are used more quickly as the temperature rises.

PESTS AND DISEASES

The warm sheltered conditions can encourage pests, especially on exotic container plants. Groups of plants raise the humidity and the danger of diseases. Fortunately, you will become aware if anything is wrong much sooner than in the open garden, especially if you make a point of inspecting the plants every few days. The more plants you have, the quicker both pests and diseases will find them and the quicker they will spread.

As already mentioned, there are only about four main pests that are likely to trouble patio plants in general – slugs, aphids (greenfly and blackfly), whitefly and red spider mite – and the answers are the same as already recommended for the open-ground plants on page 31. But it is possible that container plants could also be attacked by two other pests. Bay trees and house plant types are very prone to attack by scale insect. These are small, brown 'tortoise shells' stuck to stems and leaf veins, but black sooty moulds from their secretions is often the first sign you will notice. The other pest, mealy bug, attacks these plants too but prefers fleshy plants, especially succulents. It is much easier to see because it is covered in white or slightly pink 'cotton wool', which may hide several at a time. On cacti it can be mistaken for the fluffy areoles from which their spines grow. Fortunately, both pests succumb to permethrin-based sprays.

45

·5·
Plants in Containers

It is now commonplace for nurserymen to raise mature trees over 6m (20ft) high in containers, so it should come as no surprise that any plant can be grown in a container of some kind, given suitable conditions. Naturally some may need special treatment – humidity, high temperatures – some may have no special merits and yet others may be simply impractical, because of size or excessively fast growth. But still they can all be grown in containers if necessary!

GENERAL RULES

Tender plants

The patio is naturally warmer than the rest of the garden so a much wider range of plants can be grown than in the open soil. Containers, at least the smaller ones, can be easily moved so more tender plants can be taken inside if the weather threatens to be cold. A word of warning though – don't try to grow plants that are too tender for your area if you are unable to move them inside.

Conditions

Growing plants in containers on a patio does not make them special 'patio plants' ready to tolerate whatever conditions you or the environment wish to inflict upon them. Ferns will still prefer cool, light shade; busy lizzies warm, humid half-shade; camellias north or west-facing positions; clematis cool feet and a sunny head; maples shelter from cold winds; begonias sun, and primulas constant moisture.

Consider your plants' likes and dislikes from the start and move their containers if possible, when weather conditions change or as shade, sun or wind move with the seasons. Large immovable containers will need careful thought before siting.

Clean and healthy

Choose plants that are healthy and vigorous with no obvious signs of pests and diseases. A good nurseryman will not object to you looking at the roots before you buy. Large roots growing through the drainage holes shows starvation and irregular watering and plants seldom completely recover fully from such ill treatment. Neither will they grow successfully with the pot and compost crammed with roots. Some compost should be visible between the roots, the newer ones of which should be white.

Make sure plants in containers have been grown in containers, and not merely dug up and offered for sale in a pot. Container-grown plants will look established with firm soil and they should lift out complete with compost and root ball (Fig. 14).

Hardy evergreen trees and shrubs

Permanent, evergreen plants soften the hard lines of the patio even in winter and are valuable not least for that. In containers, just as in open ground, they slow almost to a stop during winter so they can be moved to less exposed places, which will benefit the plants and allow you to enjoy them more from the window.

Broad-leaved evergreens must be represented first by camellias. The dark glossy green of *Camellia japonica* is sparsely splashed with yellow in the variety 'Donckelaeri' and *Camellia × williamsii* 'Donation' has so many flowers that its smaller serrated leaves are often obscured in early spring. Camellias and the *Erica* family – heather, *Rhododendron*, *Pieris* and *Enkianthus* – all need acid soil or an ericaceous compost, which does not contain lime.

For less fussy evergreens try *Aucuba japonica* 'Crotonifolia', *Euonymus japonicus* 'Ovatus Aureus' and the underrated golden privet *Ligustrum ovalifolium* 'Aureum'. Hardy conifers introduce blue to the scene with such vivid dwarfs as *Picea pungens* 'Montgomery', while *Cryptomeria japonica* 'Compacta' turns from summer green to a winter purple-green haze.

Hardy deciduous trees and shrubs

Bare branches in winter may not offer the same attraction as evergreen foliage but both *Magnolia stellata*, with silver furred flower buds, and *Rhus cotinus*, perhaps with the dried candles of last summer's flowers, both make an attractive oriental tracery without their leaves. Acers, too, and the Japanese maples in particular – *Acer palmatum* and *Acer japonicum* – have elegant slender branches and beautiful, distinctive, open foliage casting only light shade.

Not-so-hardy shrubs and trees

When it is possible to protect plants by putting them under cover or taking them indoors during winter, the selection broadens considerably.

First, the borderline cases – almost hardy enough to stand any winter weather. This category includes fuchsias like 'Mrs Popple', 'Dr. Foerster' and 'Genii', and the species *Fuchsia magellanica* 'Alba' with tiny hint-of-pink white flowers. *Hydrangea macrophylla* 'Blue Wave' is a favourite too.

Evergreen, almost-hardy trees and shrubs include the Mexican orange blossom (*Choisya ternata*), *Griselinia littoralis*, a lovely soft lime green all year round, and the strawberry tree

Fig. 14 The different ways both deciduous and evergreen plants are supplied.

(a) Container-grown. Lifted autumn or spring. Grown for at least one season in container. Plant any time of year.

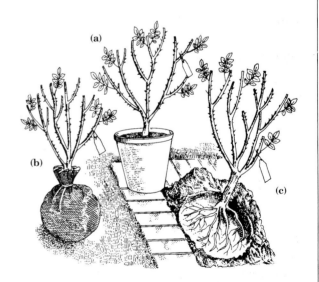

(b) Root-balled. Lifted/planted autumn or spring. Roots with soil attached wrapped in sacking/hessian.

(c) Bare root. Lifted/planted autumn. Roots usually protected in sacking or polythene (e.g. roses).

47

(*Arbutus unedo*), with lily-of-the-valley flowers and 'strawberry' fruits at the same time.

Tender evergreen plants in order of hardiness are *Myrtus communis*, white star-like flowers and typical myrtle scent; *Osmanthus heterophyllus* 'Aureomarginatus', with yellow-edged holly-like leaves and white scented flowers in autumn; and *Desfontainea spinosa*, with similar foliage but yellow-tipped, red tubular flowers in summer.

CLIMBERS AND TRAILERS

Climbing and trailing plants in containers have the advantage of mobility but they also create a different style and dimension to rigid upright plants, providing change and temporary screening (if they have support).

Perennial climbers
An ornamental vine such as *Vitis vinifera purpurea* can be as restricted as much or as little as you like. The common passion flower (*Passiflora caerulea*) does not object to the same treatment but flowers better if fed sparingly. *Wisteria sinensis* can be trained or allowed to romp, too. The herbaceous climbing sweet pea (*Lathyrus latifolius*) and flame flower, *Tropaeolum speciosum*, look best rambling over a dark evergreen.

Annual climbers
Black-eyed Susan (*Thunbergia alata*) is a vigorous annual with masses of black-eyed, orange flowers – fine pea netting makes an ideal support. Morning glory (*Ipomoea purpurea*) is now sky blue, white, pink, cerise and striped, looking like a beautiful but controllable bindweed. Cup-and-saucer vine (*Cobaea scandens*) has a white variety, 'Alba'. The ordinary one is deep purple.

◄ **Climbers do not have to go up – *Clematis macropetala*.**

Climbing annuals make an excellent temporary screen and allow maximum light through in winter.

49

Trailers

Some climbers flop quite happily and also make good trailers. The annual nasturtium is one of these and so is clematis, but only the large-flowered hybrids, as the species tangle worse than any other plant.

Real trailing plants are few and far between, but creeping Jenny (*Lysimachia nummularia*) is a good example. However, there are plenty of short trailers to make up for this – numerous campanulas like *C. portenschlagiana* and the slightly tender *C. isophylla*. Petunias have been specially bred for this effect. *Euphorbia myrsinites* is a perennial which flops well with milky blue leaves and lime green/yellow flowers; and the queen of the short trailers must be the evening primrose species *Oenothera missouriensis*.

HERBACEOUS PERENNIAL FLOWERS

Strictly speaking, herbaceous perennials grow from a root, or 'crown', beneath the soil and die down again each autumn. There are a few

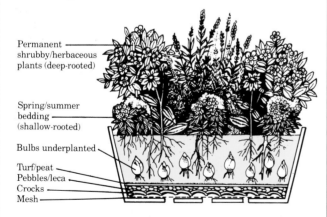

Permanent shrubby/herbaceous plants (deep-rooted)

Spring/summer bedding (shallow-rooted)

Bulbs underplanted

Turf/peat
Pebbles/leca
Crocks
Mesh

Fig. 15 To give year-round interest and colour in a deeper container, a permanent framework with bulbs underplanted and temporary colour from bedding in season. The bulbs can be left from year to year.

evergreen or semi-evergreen ones, which have the obvious advantage of year-round attraction, but the majority disappear in winter, so there are special implications when thinking about them for containers.

Special points

Most obviously, the container will appear empty in winter and it is therefore a good idea to use a mixture of evergreen and herbaceous plants, perhaps with bulbs to give winter/spring colour (Fig. 15).

Most hardy herbaceous perennials are completely hardy but, above ground in a container, the roots can become more easily frozen and they may not be quite so reliable. A good local gardener or nurseryman will be able to tell you which plants are most vulnerable in your area. Taller herbaceous plants are very likely to need some form of support. One cane behind, or among the plants, with green string looped around them and tied to the cane at both ends, is unobtrusive. If the cane will not stand firmly, in a shallow container for instance, tie it to the outside of the pot with plastic-covered garden wire. Alternatively, Link Stakes or other special wire supports can be used.

Growing in a confined space, herbaceous plants will need splitting up (dividing) about every third year, depending on the size of the pot. This risks

· YEAR-ROUND BULB COLOUR ·

Name	Description
● SPRING	
Anemone (*Anemone blanda* 'Radar')	Deep carmine red with white centre
Crocus (*Crocus 'Snow Bunting'*)	Scented; white with mustard-yellow centre
Daffodil (*Narcissus* 'Mount Hood')	Milk-white; long-lasting
Hyacinth (*Hyacinthus orientalis* 'City of Haarlem')	Fragrant; pale yellow
Narcissus (*Narcissus* 'Actaea')	Glistening white with orange-trimmed yellow cup
Greigii tulip (*Tulipa* 'Dreamboat')	Red, amber and yellow
● SUMMER	
Allium (*Allium narcissiflorum*)	Purple-pink; pendulous
Crinum lily (*Crinum powellii*)	Large funnel-shaped, pink
Golden-rayed lily (*Lilium auratum*)	Fragrant; wide; white with central orange band and red spots
Pineapple flower (*Eucomis comosa*)	Greenish-pink; tall spotted stem
● AUTUMN	
Belladonna lily (*Amaryllis belladonna*)	Funnel-shaped pink flowers before leaves
Colchicum (*Colchicum aggripinum*)	Dark chequered, bright pink; crocus-like
Cyclamen (*Cyclamen hederifolium*)	Small pink or white
Naked ladies (*Nerine bowdenii*)	Glistening pink; reflexed
Sternbergia (*Sternbergia lutea*)	Bright yellow 'crocus'
● WINTER	
Aconite (*Eranthis hyemalis*)	Butter yellow
Iris (*Iris histrioides*)	Pale china blue
Species crocus (*Crocus imperati*)	Purple stripes
Snowdrop (*Galanthus elwesii*)	White, green-tipped

damaging the roots of other plants in the container but a way round it is to grow the herbaceous plants in pots and 'plunge' them in the container up to their necks. They can then be removed quite easily, and replaced too.

Herbaceous plants can also quickly run out of both water and food, which will stunt their growth and make them flower less satisfactorily, so keep them well watered and fed.

Potted herbaceous borders
Herbaceous borders have a reputation for looking at their best in mid-summer, but the right plants will give flowers most of the spring and summer and have attractive foliage for much longer.

Starting in winter, hellebores are evergreens considered to be herbaceous. The first, *Helleborus niger* (the Christmas rose) actually seldom flowers at Christmas but, once settled in, is reliable in mid-winter. In a container, especially with overhead protection, the flowers are free from the mud splashes they get in the open ground. The native stinking hellebore, *Helleborus foetidus*, flowers in winter too. It does not actually smell and has lime-green, red-edged flowers which last for months, changing shape as the seed pods in the centre ripen. A little later, in early to mid-spring, the Lenten rose (*Helleborus orientalis*) can be pale green to almost black, with various shades of pink and plum between. No hellebores like moving and are best established alone in a large pot. A really architectural plant is *Helleborus corsicus*, with green flowers but large-toothed leaves all year round.

For a shady place and moist, ericaceous compost the false spikenard, *Smilacina racemosa*, heads the list with its tall stems of light green leaves, feathery cream flowers in summer and red fleshy fruits. Dutchman's breeches or bleeding heart, *Dicentra spectabilis*, has ferny foliage, red and pink or white flowers exactly the shape the common name suggests, while astilbes have feathery foliage and fluffy flowers. The bear's breeches, *Acanthus spinosus*, has an imposing flower spike clothed with leafy bracts which accentuates its deeply cut dark green leaves, but will need a large, deep container.

Hostas have such a variety of leaf shapes and colours – blue, green, yellow, white – and are so popular, that it is impossible to leave them out. Many flower, too, with tall spikes of blue, lilac or white. They need very moist soil and watch out for climbing slugs.

At the end of the year the Japanese anemones, *Anemone hupehensis* or *A. hybrida*, come into flower in pink and white but they have handsome maple-like foliage all summer too. These attributes also apply to floppy, wandering *Geum × borisii* with flowers of bright orange and red.

SWITCH TO BULBS

Bulbs bring a different atmosphere to the patio – crocuses breaking the spell of winter, tulips heralding summer, sophisticated lilies through the summer and autumn, *Nerine* into winter. From cheerful to exotic and, in containers, mobile too.

Use separate pots to plant daffodil, tulip and hyacinth bulbs on a layer of compost, or bulb fibre, as closely packed as possible without actually touching. Cover the bottom layer with another bed of compost and space a second layer of bulbs between the 'noses' of the bottom ones, for twice as many flowers.

In mixtures with other plants, bulbs can be planted permanently, if the container is large enough, deep down below the bedding plants that can be added later. Bulbs can also be 'plunged' in pots and removed after flowering. This is a particularly good idea in an alpine bed or trough so the bulbs can be lifted out, split up and replanted as necessary.

Bulbs like to be fed – those planted in bulb fibre particularly – and they will recover much more quickly when planted out in the garden.

ALPINE OR ROCK PLANTS

As well as sink gardens, shallow troughs and long, low raised beds, any shallow, broad pot – alpine gardeners call them 'pans' – can make a healthy home for an alpine. All that is needed is to pay a little extra attention to the drainage beneath the

► Rock gardens and scree beds are a very attractive alternative to low walls for changing levels.

◄ Alpines and dwarf conifers are ideally suited to sink gardens – although real, rough stone ones like this may be difficult to come by.

compost and to plant the alpines firmly but carefully, ensuring their crowns (the slightly raised centre of most plants that the leaves grow from) is level with the soil surface or even slightly above. Then spread fine gravel or granite chips all over the soil surface right up to the plant crown. This careful planting and chipping mulch is to help prevent 'collar' rots which alpines are prone to away from their mountain homes.

Feeding
Alpines need very little feeding – an occasional half strength dose of soluble high-potash plant food – but keep them evenly moist throughout the summer and protect them from excessive wet in the winter.

Bedding in containers
Winter, spring and summer bedding in containers is just like open-ground growing; the only difference is that watering is even more important, if that is possible, than for other container plants. If they are allowed to become too dry the plants often react by producing a final furious flourish of flowers in an attempt to set seed before they die!

Unfortunately, quickly watering as soon as you notice they are dry is not sufficient to prevent it so they must be kept evenly moist at all times. Dead-heading to keep them flowering is rather more important than in open ground, too, and virtually no other plants respond as well as bedding to thorough weekly feeding with a high-potash, soluble plant food.

ANNUALS

Annuals involve rather more work than perennials as they have to be grown from seed or bought as plants and re-planted every year. But the main drawback where containers are concerned is that they must be grown separately or with plants that do not mind some annual disturbance to their roots. However, their beautiful colours and shapes easily make up for these minor difficulties and, as a bonus, the sheltered conditions suit many more tender ones – *Schizanthus*, the poor man's orchid, comes instantly to mind!

Schizanthus start with the dwarf 'Hit Parade' at 30cm (12in) and ends with the 'Giant Hybrids' at 1.2m (4ft) or more, and by judicious sowing in autumn and spring, can be in flower most of the summer.

Other taller annuals include the deep shades and veined petals of *Salpiglossis sinuata* 'Bolero', pink or white *Lavatera trimestris* 'Silver Cup' or 'Mont Blanc', the deep purple-pink of *Malope trifida* – all between 60cm and 90cm (2 and 3ft) high.

The tobacco plant, *Nicotiana alata*, comes in almost every colour and shade but blue, many scented in the evening and perfect for containers. *Salvia splendens* 'Blaze of Fire' is an old favourite but the newer variety *S.s.* 'Lady in Red' is more open in shape and, dead-headed as soon as the main spike has faded, will produce more flowers well into autumn.

The medium size range includes *Convolvulus tricolor* 'Blue Flash', an annual cousin of the bindweed; the lady's slipper, *Calceolaria* 'Bikini' or 'Any time' series; and baby-blue-eyes *Nemophila menziesii*, which is also a fast-growing spreader.

Annual perennials

The petunia is really a perennial raised from seed each year and there are now striped and picotee versions, like the 'Star' and 'Picotee' series. Bedding geraniums (pelargoniums) are perennials which are easily kept indoors through the winter. The castor oil plant, *Ricinus communis*, is another, and the variety *R.c.* 'Impala' has deep bronze maple leaves and bright red prickly seed pods. Sophistication comes from the perennial sage, *Salvia farinacea* 'Victoria' – intense blue spikes held above grey sage foliage.

House plants on the patio

Many of our common house plants benefit from a summer rest out of doors. The greater temperature fluctuation, humidity and light intensity ripen the plants and encourage better flowering – the Christmas and Easter cacti (*Zygocactus truncatus* and *Rhipsalidopsis gaertneri*) are good examples of this. But only in mid-summer can most areas be guaranteed frost free, so it is best to err on the side of safety wherever you are.

Pelargoniums, *Abutilon pictum* and asparagus fern are all commonly grown outside, but others not so obvious are the palms like *Howea* and *Trachycarpus*, and the similar yuccas, draceanas and cordylines.

Fat-headed lizzies (×*Fatshedera lizei*) and the many forms of ivy (*Hedera helix*) are generally varieties of the hardy plants. But still proceed with care – they are used to the protection of the living-room and the variegated ones tend to be slightly less hardy.

·6·
Fruit and Vegetables in Containers

Beds and borders, planting stations and island beds within the patio, can be planted with fruit and vegetables just as easily as they can with flowering plants, shrubs and trees – even mixed in with them. In containers on the patio, the same rules apply: it is perfectly possible to grow just about any kind of vegetable or fruit. Some may not be as practical as others – loganberries or cauliflowers for instance are simply not economical in terms of space. But if loganberries or cauliflower are what you crave, and there is nowhere else to grow them but in a patio container, by all means have a go!

GENERAL RULES

Watering and feeding
Using a suitable compost and ensuring they do not go without the right food and adequate water is even more vital to fruit and vegetables than ornamental plants, because it will not only affect how much they produce but, even more importantly, their flavour.

Good taste
Flavour is, of course, a very important consideration but it can vary so much with growing conditions. Initially, at least, it is probably best to select on the basis of other people's recommendations.

Reliability is probably just as important as flavour, and a combination of both is best. 'James Grieve' is a reliable cropping apple of good flavour and a better bet than the superb flavour of 'Cox's Orange Pippin' when you consider you are likely to have fruit on the Cox only one year in three!

Lastly, that protected environment once again offers the opportunity to grow something a little more exotic. Perhaps a globe artichoke (*Cynara scolymus*), a great, grey-leaved 1.2–1.5m (4–5ft) stately specimen vegetable, not totally hardy in the coldest areas; or a 'Brown Turkey' fig, normally reliable only on warm walls in the south.

Small is beautiful

● *Soft plants* Choosing the more compact heavier-cropping varieties, which have been specially bred over recent years, makes excellent sense on the patio, especially in containers. Dwarfing by judicious pruning is also a good idea to keep plants within bounds. Normally tall-growing tomatoes can be pinched out at any height, making them just as dwarf as the special bush varieties. Runner beans pinched out regularly will climb as high, or stay as bushy as space allows.

● *Woody plants* Fruit trees are reduced in vigour by the size of their container but mainly by the

rootstock they are grafted on to, which literally stunts the growth of the variety joined to it. There are several of these rootstocks which have varying effects, and grafting the fruit variety on to them is a skilled job, so it is essential to get them from a reputable specialist supplier. They are not cheap and the aim is to have them for several years, so go for quality from the start.

Buying seed

Unlike flowers, all seed of edible plants must conform to strict international standards on type, purity and germination. However, for the small numbers of plants needed on the patio, it is undoubtedly best to buy seed packed in foil sachets from one of the reputable garden suppliers.

Buying fruit and vegetable plants

There are three rules for buying fruit and vegetable plants which really apply to all plants, whether for the open ground or containers:

1. They must be healthy. This means compact, and green. Not straggly, flopping or yellowing.

2. No obvious pests and diseases.

3. Good healthy white roots not overfilling the pot.

Ask the nurseryman to take plants out of pots or containers. Good growers won't object to this. A few small roots growing through the drainage holes is no cause for concern, but large roots show starvation and irregular watering.

Two other points to ponder are correct labelling and plants being offered for sale at the right time. A wrongly labelled variety and frost damage to tender plants are both faults that can be avoided by using a reputable nurseryman.

◄ **This sheltered corner provides the sort of suntrap necessary for growing citrus fruit on the patio.**

THE RIGHT SOIL

Fruit and vegetables fit into two principal categories – short term and long-term. Each needs slightly different growing soil or compost for the best results.

● *Short-term crops* include all vegetables grown from seed, and strawberries. The general-purpose, soil-less composts suit this category well but need extra food after about six weeks.

● *Long-term crops* are the herbs and fruit trees which need the structure of soil to keep the correct balance of air and water around their roots for what could be years. John Innes potting compost No. 3 is ideal but relatively expensive and very heavy. However, soil-less potting composts can certainly be used and the more substantial ones are usually specially labelled for tree and shrub use.

Sowing

All seed needs a firm level surface for sowing (Fig. 16). Even tiny bumps and hollows are dry windswept hills and damp, waterlogged valleys to seeds and neither is good for germination.

Water before sowing. Stand the tray or pot in shallow water until the surface is barely moist, then remove and drain immediately.

Read the packet instructions. Sow the seed thinly and evenly and, if necessary, cover to a depth about twice its size, with coarse sifted compost or sand.

Keep seed covered and warm, but not too warm, until the very first shoot appears. Then keep them in full light until ready for transplanting.

When seedlings have four leaves they are carefully dug out, holding them by the top leaves only (Fig. 17). Plant them firmly but gently in new compost, and water using a very fine rose. Keep them cool and shaded for a day or two until they start growing again.

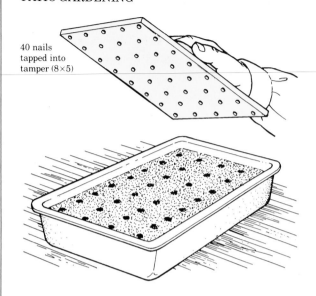

40 nails
tapped into
tamper (8×5)

Fig. 16 A flat board the same size as a seed tray, with nails in its under-surface and a handle on the back, firms compost evenly in trays and marks seed or seedling positions.

Fig. 17 Pricking out seedlings with a home-made notched dibber ('lolly stick') and a pencil to make holes. Handle seedlings by their leaves, not by their stems.

PLANTING OUT

Water all container plants at least an hour before transplanting and keep bare-rooted plants, or those which are newly dug, moist and well wrapped until ready for planting.

The main objective in moving plants is to give them more space to grow and to do it with as little damage as possible so that they recover quickly. In the case of fruit and vegetables, keeping this 'transplant shock' to a minimum is one of the skills in helping the plants to produce the maximum crop in as short a time as possible.

Logically, therefore, growing plants in containers from the start, is best for fruit and vegetables. They can then be carefully removed from one pot and transferred to the next with a complete pot-shaped rootball and no disturbance at all.

The cardinal rule of watering again after planting, to settle the compost naturally around the rootball, still applies.

Aftercare
After planting, move smaller, more mobile containers to a shady sheltered site, or shade the larger ones from direct sun for a few days, as this takes a little more shock out of the procedure.

Facing the sun
All fruit and vegetables will only produce the best crops with plenty of sunlight. Even grapes need good light and only the earliest varieties will ripen in the shade below a pergola. This means reserving south and south-west facing positions and, as far as possible, using movable containers or making larger ones more mobile with rollers or castors. The aim should be to take advantage of sunlight when necessary but also to protect plants from excessive heat, which may cause stress and force some vegetables to 'bolt', or run to seed.

·HANDY TIP·

Bury empty flower pots up to their rims in the compost at the base of vegetables and fruit and fill these at watering and feeding times. This ensures the water and food go straight to the roots. Use the largest pot the container will allow.

Shady characters

Fruit, including tomatoes in this case, will tolerate and even prefer light shade if the patio is very sheltered and warm, or the summer very bright and hot. This is especially so when fruiting heavily as they can develop deficiency diseases under these conditions.

Just as roots in containers are susceptible to freezing in winter, they are also more likely to overheat in summer. Pick positions where fruit and vegetables can keep their heads in the sun and feet in the shade.

WATERING AND FEEDING

To some extent, better flowering can be encouraged by a moderate shortage of water, but vegetables can run to seed (bolt), lose their flavour or become coarse. Once the fruit has begun to swell, problems like blossom-end-rot of tomatoes, or bitter pit of apples, can result if they are too dry for even a short time.

Vegetables

Most salad crops and green vegetables are crisper and tastier if grown quickly. By using liquid feeds, the plants can be fed at every watering with little danger of overdoing it. Soluble feeds have the advantage of being concentrated and are therefore the most economical but take care not to use too much.

Longer-term vegetables respond to a steady supply of food. In early to mid-spring use an organic like blood-fish-and-bone or one of the resin-coated slow-release types, and simply supplement this with one or two liquid feeds during summer.

Fruit

Strawberries are different to other fruit. After they have finished fruiting, cut the old leaves back and feed them well with a high-potash soluble fertilizer to build up their crowns for next year's crop. The following spring and summer, feed once or twice, using liquid high-potash again, to encourage flowering, not leaves.

·SOME VEGETABLES AND THEIR YIELDS·		
Name	Reliable standard	Container crop
● VEGETABLES		
Aubergine	'Long Purple'	$1\frac{1}{2}$–$2\frac{1}{2}$ kg (4–5 lb)
Bean		
● French	'Masterpiece'	0.1–0.2 kg ($\frac{1}{4}$–$\frac{1}{2}$ lb)
● Dwarf Runner	'Hammonds Dwarf'	0.2–0.3 kg ($\frac{1}{2}$–$\frac{3}{4}$ lb)
● Runner (pinched) (climbing)	'Scarlet Emperor'	0.5–1 kg (1–2 lb)
	'Scarlet Emperor'	0.5–1 kg (1–2 lb)
Capsicum (sweet pepper)	'Ace'	0.7–1.2 kg ($1\frac{1}{2}$–$2\frac{1}{2}$ lb)
Carrot	'Favourite'	0.2–0.5 kg ($\frac{1}{2}$–1 lb) per foot
Cucumber		
● indoor	'Telegraph Improved'	10–20
● ridge	'Burpless Tasty Green'	10–15
Kohl Rabi	'Purple Vienna'	0.1–0.3 kg ($\frac{1}{4}$–$\frac{3}{4}$ lb)
Marrow	'Green Bush'	3–5
Courgette	'Zucchini'	16–20
Potato (First Early)	'Sutton's Foremost'	0.5–1 kg (1–2 lb)
Spring cabbage	'Durham Early'	0.5–1 kg (1–2 lb)
Sweet corn	'Kelvedon Glory'	1 cob/plant
Tomato		
● Tall	'Gardeners' Delight'	$1\frac{1}{2}$–$3\frac{1}{2}$ kg
● Bush	'The Amateur'	$1\frac{1}{4}$–$2\frac{3}{4}$ kg (3 lb)
● Beefsteak	'Big Boy'	1–$2\frac{1}{2}$ kg (2–5 lb)

Apples and pears are easy to grow as dwarf bushes or trained as cordons.

Bush and tree fruit need their main high-potash feed in spring, just as they start showing signs of life – either a thorough soaking with a soluble plant food or a dry rose or tomato food gently stirred into the compost and lightly watered-in. A feed, in late summer or early autumn, with a high-potash soluble, will ripen them for winter.

PESTS AND DISEASES

Vegetable pests
Protect larger vegetable seeds before sowing with an insecticide and fungicide dust. Smaller seeds that are more thickly scattered over the compost are best watered with Cheshunt Compound the traditional copper fungicide.

Pick off caterpillars, such as the cabbage white. Rub off eggs and small colonies of aphids between the thumb and forefinger.

Slugs are a problem for which there is no simple cure. Metaldehyde or methiocarb slug pellets used sparingly are the best control. Put a few underground with potatoes when planting.

Fruit pests
An efficient way of combating pests on deciduous fruit trees and bushes is by spraying with a winter wash. Keep it away from growing plants but spray all the nooks and crannies in fences and other wood as well – pests do not lay their eggs only on plants!

Sawfly grubs look like caterpillars and, like them, can be picked off.

For pests that escape notice until the damage is done, a quick-acting, short-lived insecticide like malathion, an organic based on good old soft soap, or a spray, which uses the plant extract pyrethrum, are perhaps the best answer.

Diseases
The commonest disease on the patio will be mildew on both vegetables and fruit. On the other hand, grey mould will mostly attack vegetables because they are usually grown closer together.

There are no truly organic fungicides and while natural sulphur is of some benefit, the best treatment for both these diseases available to the gardener is a carbendazim or benomyl spray.

GROWING FRUIT

Good quality fruit trees can be expected to crop from the second year and to be fully mature, producing about the maximum crop that can be expected, in about four or five years. Surprisingly, the amount of fruit from established container trees is reasonably the same for the majority of tree fruit varieties, at between 8 and 12 lbs per tree.

Apples and pears
Apples and pears need at least one other tree flowering nearby at the same time to pollinate them so it is best to grow two of each. Or grow a 'family tree' which has three or more varieties grafted onto one rootstock (Fig. 18), though the varieties are not always as reliable as those recommended in the chart on page 62.

Cherries, peaches, nectarines and apricots
The cherries, peaches, nectarines and apricots pollinate themselves, so only one of each is necessary to get fruit. But they flower earlier than apples and will still need to be hand pollinated, especially the peaches and nectarines.

Figs
Figs are better in pots than in the open ground as they fruit more reliably when their roots are restricted. Small fruits form in the autumn and the plants will need protection in winter to make these ripen the following year.

Grapes

In a 30 or 38cm (12 or 15in) pot, grapes are easy, as pruning consists of simply cutting back all last year's growth to just one bud, then pinching off the new soft shoots three leaves after the flower bunches.

·FRUIT IN CONTAINERS·

Fruit	Variety	Description
Apples	'James Grieve'	Reliable; early
	'Discovery'	Early; superb flavour
	'Fiesta'	Similar to Cox; heavy crop
	'Sunset'	Very like Cox; heavy crop
Apricot	'Moorpark'	Reliable, good flavour
	'Farmingdale'	Heavy crop; excellent flavour; ripens early
Cherry	'Stella'	Good flavour
	'Compact Stella'	As 'Stella', less vigorous
	'Morello'	Acid cherry
Figs	'Brown Turkey'	Fairly large, rich-flavoured fruit
	'White Marseilles'	Large, sweet fruit with white flesh
Grapes (outdoor)	'Siegerebe'	White; wine or dessert
	'Müller Thurgau'	White; reliable; only average for dessert
Nectarine	'Lord Napier'	Reliable, heavy crop; early
	'Early Rivers'	Heavy crop; good flavour; very early
Peach	'Rochester'	Reliable; firm and juicy
	'Peregrine'	Superb flavour
	'Duke of York'	Juicy, delicious
Pears	'Conference'	Reliable, juicy
	'Onward'	Excellent flavour
	'Beth'	Regular fruiting; melting texture
Plum	'Denniston's Superb'	Sweet and heavy crop
	'Victoria'	Reliable; heavy crop
	'Oullin's Golden Gage'	Large, medium-sweet fruit

Dessert grapes are the best choice, as pot-grown vines are much too small to carry enough grapes for wine.

Kiwi fruit

Kiwi fruit (*Actinidia chinensis*) is very vigorous indeed and needs both a male and a female plant in a container at least 60cm (2ft) wide. They will usually only do well in warmer areas.

Melon

Melons are simple to grow but need warmth to ripen well outdoors. A warm wall, with provision for training on strings and some method of covering the plants will ensure success. Pollinate female flowers like marrows.

THE VEGETABLES

Aubergine – egg plant

The aubergine needs much the same treatment as tomatoes, but rather warmer if possible. Recommended varieties: 'Long Purple', 'Black Prince'.

Beans

Grow runner beans up 'wigwams' of canes attached to pots or pinch out to keep bushy. Recommended varieties: French – 'Masterpiece' and 'Kinghorn Wax'; Dwarf Runner – 'Hammonds Dwarf' and 'Pickwick'; Runner – 'Scarlet Emperor', 'Polestar', 'Durham Early' and 'Spring Hero'.

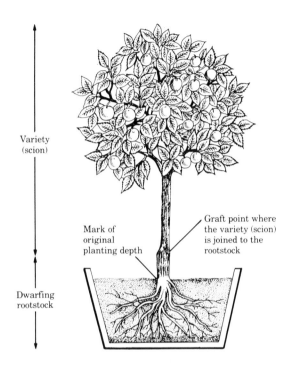

Variety
(scion)

Dwarfing
rootstock

Mark of
original
planting depth

Graft point where
the variety (scion)
is joined to the
rootstock

Fig. 18 Tree fruit in container. Plant carefully to same depth as in the nursery, with graft point well above compost.

Capsicum – sweet pepper

Grow like aubergines. Try multi-coloured 'Carnival Mixed' from Marshalls. Recommended varieties: 'Ace' and 'Redskin'.

Carrot

Pull young and tender. Sow every two weeks in same container. Recommended varieties: 'Favourite' and 'Amsterdam Forcing'.

Kohl rabi

Good for growing between other crops. Recommended varieties: 'Purple Vienna' and 'Rowel'.

Marrow and courgette

Flowers must be hand pollinated. Squash, custard marrow and vegetable spaghetti are all similar.

Recommended varieties: Marrow 'Green Bush' and 'Early Gem'; Courgette 'Zucchini' and 'Gold Rush'.

Sweet corn

Make sure the pollen gets from the tassels down to the cob by shaking the plants. Recommended varieties: 'Kelvedon Glory' and 'Early Xtra Sweet'.

Tomatoes (Fig. 19)

Regular, even watering is vital. Limit beefsteak varieties to four trusses. Recommended varieties: (Tall) 'Gardeners' Delight' and 'Sweet 100'; (Bush) 'The Amateur' and 'Red Alert'; (Beefsteak) 'Big Boy' and 'Dombito'.

Fig. 19 Tomatoes have a variety of growth habits.

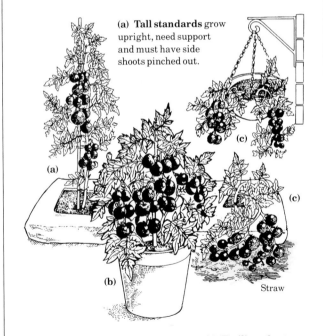

(a) Tall standards grow upright, need support and must have side shoots pinched out.

(a)

(b)

(c)

Straw

(b) Bush plants are naturally shorter and sturdy. No support needed. Don't pinch out side shoots.

(c) Trailing plants are like floppy bush plants. No support needed. Don't pinch out side shoots.

63

SALAD CROPS

Cucumber
Hand pollinate ridge (outdoor) types, unless they are all-female varieties. Recommended varieties: 'Burpless Tasty Green' and 'Bush Champion'.

Lettuce
Cut-and-come-again and the small varieties make the best use of space. Useful for growing between other plants. Recommended varieties: 'Little Gem' and 'Red Salad Bowl'.

Radish
Even watering essential. Lightly shade (including compost) in summer. Recommended varieties: 'French Breakfast' and 'Long White Icicle'.

Spinach
Keep well supplied with water. Recommended varieties: 'Sigmaleaf' and 'Symphony'. 'Sigmaleaf' is a summer and winter variety.

This bush tomato 'Totem' has been specially bred for patio growing.

Spring onion
Useful for growing with other salads. 'Ishikura' stays slim and picks over a long period. Recommended varieties: 'White Lisbon' and 'Ishikura'.

HERBS

Considering the great variety of plants we use as culinary herbs, from Mediterranean rosemary to soft green native chives, it is quite surprising that, by and large, the vast majority are perfectly happy in very similar growing conditions.

The conditions herbs revel in are simply good drainage and plenty of sun, although one or two, like angelica (*Angelica archangelica*), chives (*Allium schoenoprasum*) and mint (*Mentha spicata*), will tolerate some shade. As long as the soil is reasonable and lets water drain away easily, so that they are never too wet and can be watered freely, they will be perfectly happy.

Feeding should be limited to a light spring dressing and an occasional summer watering with soluble high-potash plant food. The reason is that most aromatic herbs seem to hold their scent and flavour better if they are grown a little 'hard'.

Growing herbs in a special bed is the traditional recommendation. This is certainly practical, and translates very well to a pot or container of some kind. Even a giant like fennel is a pot-plant possibility, especially the dark bronze-leaved variety *Foeniculum vulgare* 'Purpureum', an eyecatching 1.5m (5ft) feathery column, giving off a wonderful aniseed scent every time you pick it or brush past.

Basil, thyme, marjoram (oregano), parsley, and especially mint, which tends to take over if given the freedom of the open soil, are all easily grown in pots. A trough of mixed herbs by the kitchen door is handy for picking, with the bonus of scent wafting indoors on a warm summer afternoon.

Herbs revel in the freely drained compost and open sunny conditions a window box on a south-facing sill can provide.

Seeds or plants

Most herbs can easily be grown from seed. Basil, dill, summer savory and borage (if you consider it a herb), are annuals and caraway, chervil, clary and parsley are biennials.

Shrubby herbs, like rosemary, bay, sage and rue are best bought as young plants or rooted from summer cuttings.

Balm, fennel and tarragon are herbaceous perennials you can buy from a nursery.

Mixed border

Consider growing herbs as ornamental plants too. Fennel, which has already been mentioned as a pot plant, makes a good border plant. Thyme comes in golden, silver and variegated-leaved varieties (*Thymus×citriodorus* 'Aurea', 'Silver Posie' and 'Variegatus') which all flower, and the golden or purple-leaved sages, (*Salvia officinalis* 'Icterina' and 'Purpurea') also have tall spikes of mauve flowers. Angelica makes an unusual soft green plant in a wild corner and, of course, parsley makes a fine edging plant anywhere in the garden.

Hanging Baskets

Hanging baskets have become an almost essential addition to the summer patio, but be careful not to overdo the effect. Remember, too, that hanging baskets use a lot of water and need more at least once, if not twice, a day, which can be all too easy to forget when you're busy. The most effective way to water is to take the basket down and soak it in a bowl of water until the compost is evenly moist throughout. However, there are available lowering devices for use when watering – see p. 70.

LOCATION

Since it is not essential to test a hanging basket with a finger to discover if it needs water – you can always assume that it will – they do not need to be as accessible as other containers. They can decorate walls, beams, arches, pergolas. They can be hung each side of a door or window, provided that leaning out of the latter to water, feed or deadhead, is not dangerous.

Remember to keep them high – well above head height (Fig. 20) – and away from seats and furniture where they could drip on people or food, or, just as important, on to plants below which may be damaged by water or liquid plant food running through. But don't hang them too high either. Unless part of a scheme or plan, an isolated basket too far above eye level not only looks odd but presents additional problems for watering and general care.

Sun and shade

Hanging baskets are mainly used for spots of summer colour and as a general rule the more sun they get the better. So again, a south or south-west facing spot would be best.

Against a wall, one side is always shaded but this is never seen. Hanging from an overhead support there has to be a shady side and it may be necessary to turn the basket every few days to keep it growing evenly all over.

Shade plants can of course be used and, once again, the busy lizzie must be mentioned as the very best plant for light shade.

DECORATIVE BASKETS

The planned shape of the final display should be nicely rounded with tall plants at the centre, such as drooping Fuchsia 'Golden Marinka' or trailing *Geranium* 'Rouletta', smaller plants like *Petunia* 'Cascade' or the 'Imperial' series of pansies surrounding them, and creeping ones, like *Lobelia* 'Red Cascade' or *Campanula isophylla* at the edges and through the bottom (if the basket is wire or plastic mesh). The aim is to give the basket a completely covered effect.

Busy lizzies and fibrous-rooted begonias will take partial or light shade, as will most house plants. These are perennials and therefore relatively expensive so, to save money, they can be brought inside or propagated from cuttings during the winter and used again next year.

Colour full

The colour used in hanging baskets will depend very much upon the type and style of patio. Bright colours are more easily chosen but also more easily overdone as they can detract from more restful, muted shades and spoil a desired effect.

Silver-leaved cineraria with trailing ivies and soft pink busy lizzie offer a gentler picture in sun or light shade. Spiky green and white spider plants, *Chlorophytum comosum*, with purple petunias and white pansies looks well thought out, and the variegated nasturtium, *Tropaeolum majus* 'Alaska' makes an attractive background for geraniums and verbenas.

Ideas for winter

It is not an easy task to make hanging baskets colourful and interesting throughout winter as there are few perennials that will tolerate the exposure. Baskets hold only a small amount of compost, which may dry out easily in summer but just as easily freeze in winter, particularly in exposed spots or where the sun does not reach. It should also be remembered that they are more exposed to wind and rain than are, say, window boxes, so plants must be very hardy and sturdy.

However, if you cannot bear the sight of them empty all winter, variegated ives, such as the hardier *Hedera helix* 'Glacier', used as 'ground cover', with Universal pansies dotted through and between them, is one suggestion that works well.

Heathers are another idea but they take some time to establish and fill a basket, so they are probably best permanently planted. On the other hand, lightly clipped over each spring after flowering, they will last for many years. Choose some of the coloured foliage varieties, such as *Erica carnea* 'Foxhollow' with golden foliage all year round and pink flowers in winter, to take maximum advantage of them.

HANGING HARVEST

It is not usual to grow herbs, fruit or vegetables in a hanging basket but it is a novel idea and could be very practical, especially if there is a kitchen window handy or a door leading directly onto the patio.

Hanging herbs

If there is no room for a window box, why not hang one or two baskets either side of a window, or even three underneath, to make a miniature herb garden? They will certainly be easy to reach for picking and watering.

Plastic containers need to be well crocked at the bottom for drainage but, once established, would take less invasive herbs like thyme, parsley, chives or marjoram – all of which smell good and are visited by bees and butterflies. Mint needs a hanging basket of its own, so grow one of the more exciting ones – apple mint for instance.

Fig. 20 Site hanging baskets deliberately low, on pedestals or walls, *or* high – at least 15 cm (6 in) above head height to prevent accidents.

At least 15 cm (6 in)

Cherry tomatoes fruit well in hanging baskets if fed and watered regularly.

The new Busy Lizzie hybrids do not object to some shade but they can take sun too.

Hanging vegetables

For vegetables there are the newer dwarf tomatoes like 'Red Alert' and 'Tumbler', which are normally allowed to wander at will over the soil so also flop obligingly over the edges of a hanging basket.

Dwarf French or runner beans and even climbing varieties, judiciously pinched out, crop well enough and long enough to make them worth considering. But let beans and especially tomatoes dry out, even for an instant, at your peril – the very least you will get is no crop!

Strawberries

There are few fruits suited to hanging baskets. Even strawberries need considerable preparation, and should, ideally, be planted in the late summer or autumn and protected over winter if you want them to fruit in their first year.

Try varieties like 'Tenira', 'Tamella', and 'Hapil', for summer fruit and the 'perpetual' variety 'Aromel', for summer and autumn fruit. 'Baron Solemacher' is an alpine variety with no runners to make it attractive as well as practical, but it fruits in its first year from seed and produces masses of tiny fruit over a long period.

TYPES OF BASKETS

Hanging baskets, too, have changed their image over recent years. There are now, for instance, various styles and designs in plastic – white, stone or terracotta coloured and with or without clip-on watering saucers underneath (Fig. 21). There are fibre pots which can be used alone or inside other baskets. This is particularly useful for wooden ones, which are often sold in kit form, as it prevents the wood getting too wet. There is terracotta itself, of course, which is rather heavy and very breakable. The most popular hanging baskets are still those made of galvanized wire coated with

A really well grown
hanging basket will hide all
trace of the wires and moss
lining.

green, white or black plastic. These are not only the most satisfactory, as they are the most easily planted through the sides and bottom, they are also the least expensive. All these come with chains or, nowadays, plastic struts to hang them by.

Lowering devices (Fig. 22)

To bring baskets down to a convenient height for watering and feeding, various types of hanging basket pulleys are available. These work on the same principle as roller blinds, the basket being attached to a nylon cord. It can then be lowered as required, and simply raised to lock in place again.

Silver linings

Sphagnum moss is the traditional lining, and how to use this is detailed on page 73. But there are now many other choices of lining material.

As well as compressed fibre hanging baskets, there are bowls of this material, too, designed to fit

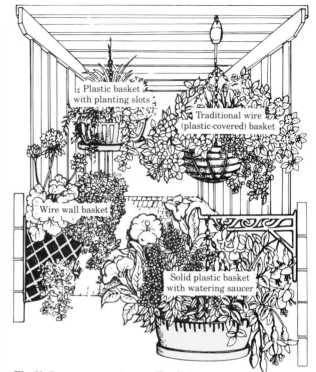

Fig. 21 **Some common types of basket.**

TRAILING VEGETABLES FOR HANGING BASKETS				
Vegetable	**Variety**	**Best points**	**Plant out**	**Growing tips**
Bean				
● French	'Blue Lake'	Climbing type; good crop	Late spring–early summer	Pinch out climbers; pick
	'Loch Ness'	Good for cold areas; bush	Late spring–early summer	regularly
	'Purple Podded Climbing'	Decorative bunches of beans	Late spring–early summer	
● Runner	'Hammonds Dwarf Scarlet'	Long season	Late spring–early summer	
Courgette	'Zucchini'	Prolific	Early summer	Use large container; pinch out growing tips; pick courgettes regularly
	'Aristocrat'	Good crop; early	Early summer	
	'Onyx'	Early	Early summer	
Cucumber	'Sweet Success'	Burp-free; seedless	Early summer	Outdoor varieties may need pollinating
	'Amslic'	Disease-resistant	Early summer	
Pea	'Sugar Snap'	Mange-tout; eat pods too	Mid–late spring	Large container; pick regularly, especially mange-tout
	'Pilot'	Early, heavy crop	Early–mid-spring	
	'Hurst Green Shaft'	Large pods; disease-resistant	Mid–late spring	
Tomato	'Red Alert'	Very early; good flavour	Late spring-early summer	No pinching out; fruit needs netting support

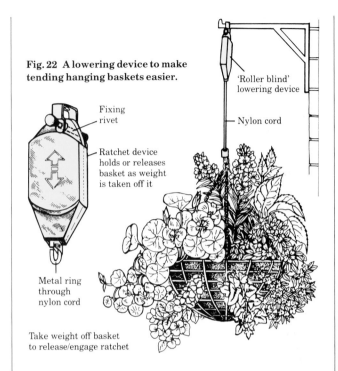

Fig. 22 A lowering device to make tending hanging baskets easier.

'Roller blind' lowering device

Fixing rivet

Nylon cord

Ratchet device holds or releases basket as weight is taken off it

Metal ring through nylon cord

Take weight off basket to release/engage ratchet

the various sized baskets. Although very solid, holes can be made through them with an apple corer, so they are quite useful for wire baskets, too.

The simplest liner, however, is a foam plastic disc with slits cut in the outside edges, which fits any basket and can be used again and again (Fig. 23).

An early start

Planning and planting hanging baskets well before hanging-out time is important so that they are properly filled with established plants and do not spend the first few weeks outdoors looking rather sparse and colourless.

The usual time to plant is mid-spring after which they must be protected from frost until they can go outside safely. For baskets with tender or half-hardy plants – begonia, pelargonium, petunia – this will not be until early summer.

Quantity and quality

It takes a bit of practice to get the perfect number without overcrowding the basket. One central plant, six surrounding ones and about ten trailers for planting through the bottom will be ample for a 30–38cm (12–15in) basket. It is best to give the plants room to grow strongly and spread naturally. Overplanting may fill the basket quickly but before very long a good third of the flowers will be hidden and deadheading will become a daily chore throughout summer.

Fig. 23 Two ways of lining and preparing a basket.

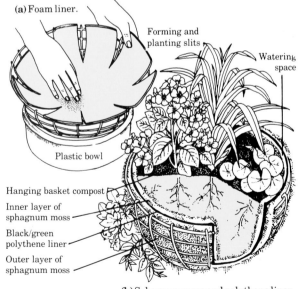

(a) Foam liner.

Forming and planting slits

Watering space

Plastic bowl

Hanging basket compost

Inner layer of sphagnum moss

Black/green polythene liner

Outer layer of sphagnum moss

(b) Sphagnum moss and polythene liner.

71

Hanging baskets are an essential part of the patio container garden.

A burgeoning hanging basket like this will need watering at least once a day throughout summer.

PLANTING

Hanging baskets with flat bottoms or watering saucers attached, stand firmly during filling and planting but round-bottomed ones will need standing in an empty seed tray or a shallow plastic bowl to keep them still.

Filling

A layer of sphagnum moss is the first step for open mesh baskets. Natural moss looks best but there are artificial ones and, even if a fibre or foam liner is used, a layer of natural moss on the outside holds quite a bit of water, helping the plants to grow more quickly through it. If moss is the main liner, put a layer of black or green polythene over this, followed by a second layer of moss, pressed in right up to the basket rim.

Compost

It is a good idea to use a special hanging basket compost, as these often contain special fertilizers and are designed to retain water more efficiently so that the plants get the maximum benefit.

Planting method

Once again, water the plants well before starting. Put a 5cm (2in) layer of compost in the bottom of the lined basket and then, in mesh or other perforated baskets, start to put in the plants. Make planting holes through the liner all round the basket and carefully tease the roots of each plant through. Put in another layer of compost and continue planting and filling in this way, pushing the compost firmly round the plants, until it is about 2.5cm (1in) from the top of the moss or liner. Leave a hole for a central main plant and put this in next, finishing off with the plants around the top (Fig. 24).

Water the basket well after planting and hang in a cool, shaded place for a few days to recover.

A lowering device attached to the hanging basket bracket makes watering much easier.

Support

The only thing to say about hanging basket supports is that they must be strong and firmly fixed. Baskets are the most hazardous containers from this point of view because all the others have some form of supporting surface underneath them. Use heavy duty screws and galvanized hooks in woodwork and make certain they are screwed well home. Drill and plug brick or stonework and use screws exactly the right size.

The chains must be checked, preferably before filling, and the hooked ends crimped onto the edges of the basket with pliers, if necessary. Wiring the three outer, hooked ends of the chain together, all facing the same way, makes for easier and safer hanging.

To make watering and feeding easier, attach a pulley to the mounting bracket, so the basket can be lowered to a convenient height and raised to lock it in place again.

PLANTS FOR HANGING BASKETS

There are so many plants that look good and grow well in hanging baskets, provided they are well fed and watered, that it is really a crime not to try some of the more unusual ones.

The plants
For key to plant type see foot of column.

Ajuga reptans (bugle) HP. Good covering plant on top and underneath. Green, bronze red and cream leaves and blue flowers.

Alchemilla mollis (lady's mantle) HP. Soft grey foliage, with lime-green fluffy flowers.

Allysum saxatile (allysum) HP. 'Compactum' is compact with bright gold spring flowers.

Anthemis nobilis (chamomile) HP. 'Treneague' is green and scented. *A. cupaniana* has ferny silver foliage all year round.

KEY	
HA	Hardy Annual
HHA	Half-Hardy Annual
HP	Hardy Perennial
HHP	Half-Hardy Perennial
TP	Tender Perennial
HSh	Hardy Shrub

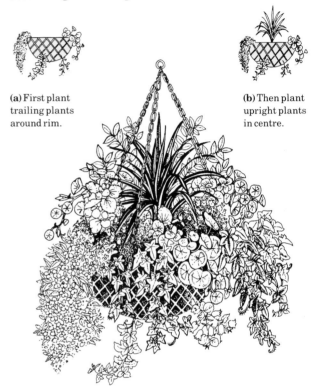

Fig. 24 **Traditional arrangement of hanging basket with central 'dot' plant for height, surrounding fillers and trailers over the edge and through the bottom.**

(a) First plant trailing plants around rim.

(b) Then plant upright plants in centre.

Arenaria balearica (arenaria) HP. Moss-like foliage and tiny white star flowers. Good 'liner'.

Armeria maritima (thrift) HP. 'Liner' to replace moss. Evergreen with pink long-stemmed flowers. Tolerant of dry conditions.

Aubrieta deltoidea (aubrieta) HP. Evergreen with blue/mauve flowers in spring. Covers basket.

Begonia × tuberhybrida (tuberous begonia) and *B. hyemalis* (rieger begonia) TP. Both produce masses of flowers throughout summer.

Campanula species (bellflower) HP, HHP. Blue or white flowers. Trailers and loose clumps.

Chlorophytum comosum 'Variegatum' (spider plant) TP. Indoors in winter, outdoors in summer.

Coleus blumei (flame nettle) TP. Richly coloured, velvety leaves.

Eccremocarpus scaber (Chilean glory flower) HHP. Normally a climber; unusual trailer. Bright orange, tubular flowers.

Euonymus fortunei (euonymus) HSh. The variety 'Emerald 'n' Gold' is a very good evergreen trailer.

Fuchsia × hybrida (fuchsia) HHP. Dwarf, tall, upright, pendulous, trailing. White, pink, red.

Geranium species (geranium) HP. Herbaceous perennials (*not* pelargoniums). Underrated foliage and flowering plants.

Glechoma hederacea (ground ivy) HP. The variety 'Variegata' with cream-splashed leaves is best. The longest trailer of all.

Hedera helix (ivy) HP. Many variegated and small-leaved varieties. Good, evergreen, basket 'ground-cover' and trailers.

Impatiens sultanii, I. petersiana, etc. (busy lizzie) HHP. The best flowering plant for shade.

Lobelia erinus (lobelia) HHA. There are now white and almost-red varieties. Very popular.

Petunia × hybrida (petunia) HA. Another traditional basket plant. Spoilt for choice – all colours, double, single, frilled, picotee, striped.

Plectranthus oertendahlii (Swedish ivy) TP. A house plant in reality but an indestructible trailing basket plant.

Thymus serpyllus (thyme) HP. Plant all round and clip after flowering. Scented.

Tradescantia fluminensis TP. Trailing house plant with green and white leaves. 'Quicksilver' is a robust variety.

Tropaeolum majus (nasturtium). HA. Variety 'Alaska' has variegated leaves.

Zebrina pendula TP. Another useful trailing plant, pink/purple, and variegated.

·FERTILIZERS FOR CONTAINER PLANTS·

Type	Description	Uses
Controlled release	Polymer-coated granules	Long-term plants; spring–early summer
Dry applied	Granules or powder	Spring base dressing; summer top-dressing
Liquid	Concentrated liquid for dilution	Continuous feeding of vegetables and fruit
Liquid Organic	Seaweed and other natural extracts	Gentle, natural stimulant for all plants
Organic	Granules or powder; blend of natural ingredients	Natural slow-release; general spring and summer use
Plant Tonic	Soluble 'Trace Element' granules	Weak or yellowing plants; early spring to late summer
Soluble	Concentrated; used in solution or as dry dressing	Best all-year round; spring and summer for flowers and fruit; late summer for perennials

·8·
Window Boxes

Window boxes are limited to windows and therefore the choice of position and aspect is largely made for you; however, if there is a choice, the most open and sunny sills are best for the greatest range of plants.

One of the main attractions of window boxes is that they give pleasure indoors as well as out, even on gloomy days when sitting on the patio is not so attractive. The opportunity of using any window sill should not, therefore, be missed.

Location
Don't forget window boxes can be sited on *or* under a ledge, even both, as long as they can be firmly fixed and easily reached – preferably from the window but, failing that, from outside. Outward-opening casement windows are limited both from the point of view of position – the box can only go underneath – and the height of the plants that can be used. This applies equally to upstairs boxes but with inward-opening, sash or other sliding windows, upstairs has the distinct plus of being able to use even taller plants without worrying so much about obliterating the view.

Long and lean
Although the maximum size of box will depend on the window sill, it looks best and is safest if it does not overhang a great deal. Ideally, it should be no wider than, and as long as, the sill and at least 20cm (8in) deep – short boxes look decidedly odd and shallow ones run out of everything too quickly. On very narrow sills, wider boxes may be the only realistic approach but in that case longer support brackets underneath, or another very secure method of fixing, will be essential for safety's sake (see page 82). The box must, of course, have drainage holes and, since sills are angled to allow rain to run off, it will also have to be set on wedges – not only because boxes do not look right leaning forward, but also to ensure the plants are evenly fed and watered. If they are not level, gravity pulls the water to the front of the box taking nutrients with it and leaving the back plants permanently too dry and short of food. Wooden wedges must be treated with preservative.

Year-round interest
In large boxes you can plan a year-round scheme using the whole range of suitable plant types – for instance, a permanent planting of ivy, aubrieta, heather and dwarf conifers, with temporary spring bulbs replaced later by summer bedding, and for winter Universal pansies, polyanthus or double daisies. A different way to make them year-round, is by keeping the plants in their pots (Fig. 25). Fill the box with moist compost or leca and plunge the pots into this up to their rims, otherwise they will dry out too quickly.

► Choose window box plants carefully avoiding taller varieties as they can obscure the window.

▼ A well-planted window box can be tidy and leave a clear view from the window.

Higher plants

Alpines are a particularly good idea for window boxes because they need little attention and are easy to tend. In fact, because they thrive on neglect, the main concern about alpines is that it is rather too easy to forget to water or feed them at all.

A KITCHEN GARDEN

Another use, particularly on a kitchen window sill, is for herbs, vegetables or, even fruit. These can be mixed with flowering plants but watering should not be neglected in hot weather. All quick-growing vegetables and salad crops need regular feeding with a liquid or soluble fertilizer.

Flavour full

Herbs are certainly a good idea. Evergreen ones look attractive all year round, too. Thyme is one of the most popular, being low-growing with small leaves and pretty mauve summer flowers. Common thyme has the strongest flavour, lemon thyme is faintly citrus, excellent for adding to sweets. There are golden-leaved forms of both.

Rosemary is a shrubby plant with blue flowers but it needs regular clipping to keep it small and will still grow to about 30cm (12in) high, so keep it to one side or it will dominate the box.

Chives are invaluable for chopping, adding an onion-flavour to salads or for decoration of savoury dishes and soups. They must be cut back almost to the ground to encourage new growth. If left to flower, chives have tufty pink blooms.

Parsley is a hardy biennial. The plain-leaved type lasts better than the curly one if it is picked regularly and not allowed to flower.

Don't grow mint in a window box unless you can't get enough of it – it will take over and swamp the other plants.

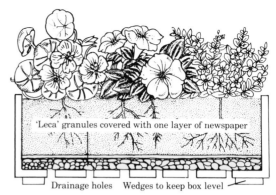

'Leca' granules covered with one layer of newspaper

Drainage holes   Wedges to keep box level

(a) Direct planting.

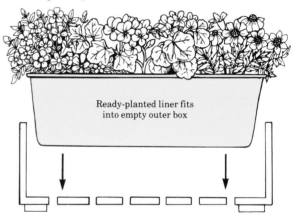

Ready-planted liner fits into empty outer box

(b) Using a liner.

Flower pots sunk in compost

(c) 'Change-over' method with pots.

Fig. 25 Three ways of planting window boxes. All boxes should have drainage holes and wedges to keep them level.

Salad days

Dwarf bush tomatoes ripen easily and reliably in the warmth from walls and the sunlight reflected from windows, and the tiniest kinds taste delicious. They do not need support unless the ledge is very windy and, just like any tomatoes, should never be allowed to become in the least dry, not even for a moment. Radish and spring onions will grow easily and so will lettuce. Of the latter, the upright cos varieties take up less room, or you might try dwarf butterheads, like 'Tom Thumb', which mature fast. Loose-leaf varieties, like 'Salad Bowl', will produce a mass of leaves for picking a few at a time without

·WINTER COLOUR FROM WINDOW BOXES·

Name	Description
Black grass (*Ophiopogon planiscapus*)	Almost-black grassy leaves
Bugle (*Ajuga reptans* 'Multicolour')	Green, cream and pink leaves all year round
Daffodil (*Narcissus* 'February Gold')	Smaller slender flowers mid–late winter
Disk-leaved hebe (*Hebe pinguifolia* 'Pagei')	Neat grey leaves all year round
English ivy (*Hedera helix* 'Glacier')	Variegated leaves all year round
Euonymus (*Euonymus fortunei* 'Emerald & Gold')	Green-gold leaves all year round
Flaky juniper (*Juniperus squamata* 'Blue Star')	Blue leaves, all year round
Hardy cyclamen (*Cyclamen coum*)	Pink flowers early winter; marbled foliage follows
Heather (*Erica carnea* 'King George')	Pink flowers in winter
Stonecrop (*Sedum spathulifolium purpureum*)	Fleshy purplish-white dusted leaves all year round
Universal pansy (*Viola×wittrockiana*);	Range of colours in winter–spring
Variegated ground ivy (*Glechoma hederacea* 'Variegata')	Trailing, variegated nettle leaves all year round
Variegated sage (*Salvia officinalis* 'Icterina')	Gold-grey leaves all year round

·HANDY TIP·

Use two or three liners which fit inside the window box exactly. Plant one for autumn and winter, one for spring and one for summer – and ring the changes. Keep the 'in waiting' ones in a good growing place to suit their contents.

taking the whole plant, and the reddish-brown variety, 'Red Salad Bowl', adds a little colour to the box and to the mixed salad.

Fruit case

The only really suitable fruit for a window box is strawberries. Plants, with the runners trailing over the edge and fruiting at the same time, look very attractive. They can be bought and planted in autumn to fruit the following summer unless the area is subject to severe winters, in which case it is best to plant them in pots indoors for the winter and plant out in spring without disturbing their roots. Or try alpine varieties which carry small succulent fruits on arching stems, crop all summer long, and are not so interesting to birds. They make tidy clumps, do not produce runners and will fruit year after year if they are kept watered and fed in the growing season. A recommended variety would be 'Baron Solemacher'.

TYPES OF WINDOW BOX

The choice of window box – elaborate and ornate or plain and simple – depends on the style of the building, the type of patio and what you want to grow. Brightly coloured or highly decorated boxes may look attractive in the shop or garden centre but can easily overpower the plants they are supposed to complement. Clean lines and neutral

Chrysanthemums and other pot plants can be put in window boxes in their pots and simply changed when they fade.

colours are safest, a matt or silk finish to match the paintwork may be the answer, although white needs annual re-painting and regular cleaning, particularly in towns. Fixed below windows, boxes also look very effective painted to match the walls, as the plants then automatically become the main feature.

● *Plastic* troughs are light but should be made from one of the tough, long-lasting plastics. Thin plastic can split and untreated types can become brittle in sunlight.

● *Wrought-iron and steel* boxes have plastic or wooden inserts but the metal must be painted every year to prevent rust which will indelibly stain sills and walls. Try to get plastic-coated iron and steel or, better still, aluminium, which is virtually corrosion free.

● *Glass fibre* is very long-lasting and makes very realistic replicas of other materials.

● *Unglazed earthenware* looks lovely, in the right setting, but it is heavy and breakable.

● *Timber, rough or planed,* is probably best because it fits in with most styles and it works out one of the least expensive materials (particularly if you make your own boxes). It can be painted but it will also look good if it is stained and/or varnished, but always paint the inside with preservative, *not* creosote. Boxes can also be given a rustic look by attaching cork bark on the front and sides.

Planting up
Pay extra attention to drainage 'crocks' and drainage holes in window boxes resting on sills and on top of other ledges and walls. When the box is installed and filled with growing plants, their drainage holes are usually inaccessible and if they become blocked, you may be faced with the difficult task of taking the box down to unblock them. Left unattended the compost at the bottom may become waterlogged and airless which will cause root rot and harm to plants. A layer of leca or other aggregate granules will help keep the drainage holes clear, and leca will also act as a reservoir. Cover this with a single layer of newspaper which will stop the compost washing down and causing a blockage.

▶ **Window boxes on narrow sills must be safely fixed. On sloping sills, level boxes with wedges.**

Use soil-less compost in preference and choose the standard potting type, even for winter plants such as heather. Most summer plants grow strongly and long-term, shrubby plants will need the initial supply of nutrients to get well established. Deciduous permanent residents do not grow at all in winter and evergreen ones only very little, so *do not* use a controlled release fertilizer after early summer, as most of them dissolve slowly all the time in moist compost and could easily release too much for the plants.

As always, water plants well before planting and again afterwards, to settle them in.

Fixtures and fittings

Next to hanging baskets, window boxes represent the greatest safety hazard if not adequately fixed in position (Fig. 26).

First make sure the boxes are level, using wedges underneath. This encourages them to stay put, not slide off!

Brackets underneath window boxes are the simplest support and with a long upper arm the ends can be bent up in front of the box to make it even more secure.

If brackets are not possible, use a metal, wood or plastic 'strap' across the front of the box, fixed to the wall each end, screws (brass or galvanized screws only) through the ends or bottom into the supporting surface, or hooks in the wall hooked into 'eyes' attached to the box. However, if there is no method of fixing them securely, don't use window boxes!

PLANTS FOR WINDOW BOXES

Window boxes are really no different to other containers except that they are always 'one sided' and tend to be rather limited in size. They are also an important intermediate step between the house

Fig. 26 Methods of attaching/fixing window boxes. Use either (a) or (b) for wide window sills and wooden frames.

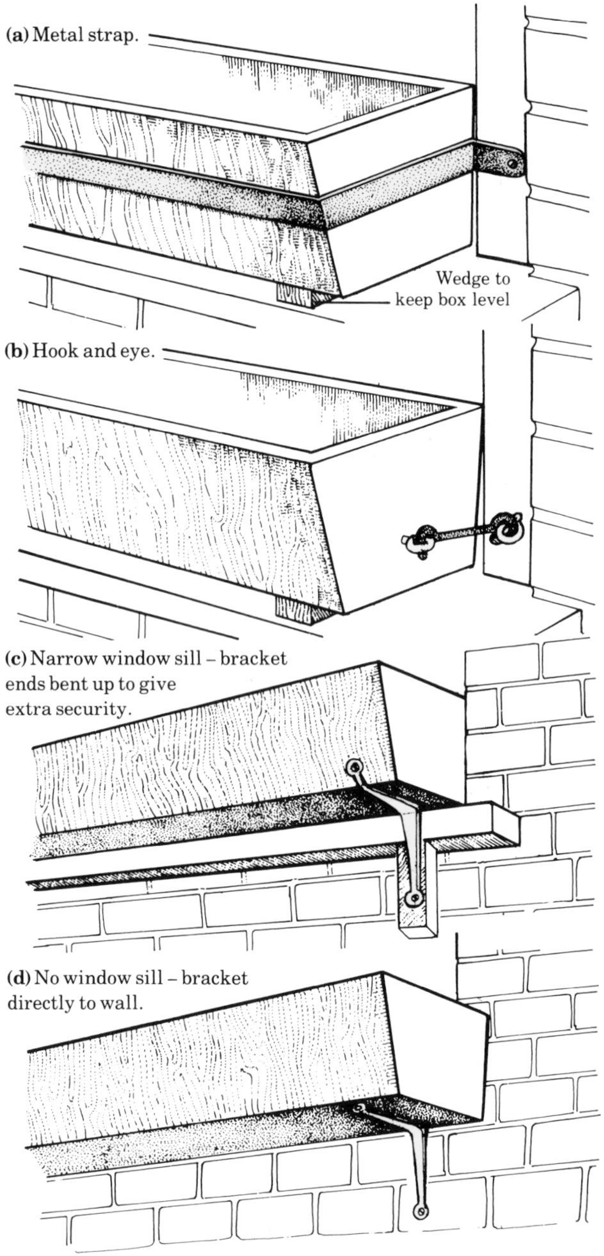

(a) Metal strap.

Wedge to keep box level

(b) Hook and eye.

(c) Narrow window sill – bracket ends bent up to give extra security.

(d) No window sill – bracket directly to wall.

·HANDY TIP·

A mirror inside the window, reflecting light onto the back of the plants will stop them leaning outwards toward the light while they are young and getting established. A board covered with silver foil has much the same effect.

and patio and are more constantly and closely in view. Therefore, although most plants recommended for small containers, particularly hanging baskets, make a good choice, others are of particular value for their length of flowering, reliability and scent. (See list and key on page 74).

Antirrhinum majus (snapdragon) HP. Dwarf snapdragons like 'Pixie' and 'Tom Thumb' flower continually if deadheaded.

Azalea obtusa (kurume azalea) HSh, Dwarf evergreen for early, pink flowers. Winter, too.

Brachycome iberidifolia (Swan River daisy) HA. Small, bushy, with spidery leaves and fragrant blue or mauve flowers.

Buxus sempervirens (box) HSh. Small plants, clipped tightly as a 'dot' plant or edging. Winter, too.

Calendula officinalis (pot marigold) HA. Short variety 'Fiesta Gitana' has cream to orange flowers.

Cheiranthus allionii (wallflower) HB. 'Spring Jester' mixed coloured dwarfs. Scented, to start the year.

Conifers. Many hundreds of dwarf varieties with blue, green, grey, and gold foliage and globular, upright, spreading flat and pendulous shapes. Winter, too.

Erica carnea/Calluna vulgaris (heath or heather) HSh. Most are very hardy. Coloured foliage all year round and flowers. Winter, too.

Grasses. Coloured leaves – golden, green, blue, striped – and many attractive seed heads.

Matthiola bicornis (night-scented stock) HA. Delicate pale lilac flowers. Strong evening perfume. Sow in the box in early spring.

Rosa chinensis minima (fairy rose) HSh. Tiny, 'real' roses 25–30 cm (10–112 in) high. Pink, red, yellow and white.

Salvia splendens (salvia) HHA. The variety 'Lady in Red' is very graceful and flowers into autumn if deadheaded.

·PLANTS SPECIALLY BRED FOR WINDOW BOXES·

Name	Description
● FRUIT AND VEGETABLES	
Cucumber 'Bush Champion'	Very compact plant; high quality fruit; even shape; good yield
Pepper 'Redskin F₁'	Only about 30 cm (12 in) high; tolerant of cool weather conditions; large fruit
Strawberry 'Temptation'	Summer variety raised from seed; fruits in same year
Tomato 'Tumbler F₁'	Only about 30 cm (12 in) high; tolerant of cool weather conditions; large fruit
● FLOWERS	
Asarina 'Victoria Falls'	Pendulous, 45 cm (18 in) semi-evergreen; pink/purple trumpet flowers
Begonia semperflorens 'All Rounder Mixed'	Prolific flowers; wind and weather-tolerant
Campanula carpatica 'Bellissimo'	Hardy perennial; blue and white flowers; long flowering period
Impatiens 'Tempo Series'	Early flowering; compact, pendulous
Petunia 'Bouquet Mixed'	Fully double flowers

·9·
Using the Patio

Gardening first started in the Middle East, probably Egypt, over four thousand years ago when, not surprisingly, the climate had much to do with the development of shaded gardens to provide a retreat from the fierceness of the summer sun. The desert's lack of water and vegetation made these essential ingredients of any garden. In addition, the vast gulf between the rulers and the ordinary people almost certainly brought about the need for privacy from prying eyes and protection from potential thieves – walls without windows facing onto the street, would undoubtedly be a deterrent.

The famed *harems* of the Arab countries are often depicted with running water and plants but, most of all, seclusion, with elaborate screens and perforated walls inside, and high walls around the outside.

The Hanging Gardens of Babylon were constructed by King Nebuchadnezzar for his wife Amytis, who came from a much kinder landscape than the deserts of southern Iraq and, naturally, was nostalgic for the greenery of her home. This homesickness became a common reason for conquerors of foreign lands to take gardens with them wherever they went – and it still is. On a much smaller scale, how many of us today cherish plants we were given by someone special or from somewhere special?

Religion also played a large part in the Moorish gardens. Mosques often have gardens attached to or associated with them and the peace and tranquillity of their enclosed gardens is synonymous with the contemplation of prayer. Even today monasteries all over the world still maintain their cloister gardens.

Food also played a part in the original development of the enclosed garden. The fields were used for staple crops like grain, olives and wine grapes, but the forerunner of the patio was used to grow the dessert grapes, as is still often the case around the Mediterranean, and not only local fruit but exotic fruit which needed more watchful attention.

But, through all these uses, the main idea of a peaceful, shaded, cool oasis still held sway – something of a far cry from today's northern European patio which still maintains its privacy but is now more of a sun trap than a shade trap and is more often than not rather noisier, with children and barbecue parties, than the quieter and more peaceful world over the fence!

MODERN USES OF PATIOS

The British patio has generally been, until recently, a place for the children to play without getting dirty, for sunbathing or just sitting out, or for the occasional 'picnic'. Admittedly, barbecues are also popular but this is really as far as it goes.

▶ **The Lion Courtyard in the Alhambra Palace in Granada is an authentic Moorish patio.**

British reticence and the weather combine to limit our vision of what the patio could be used for.

In North America, however, using the patio has developed into an art form! And there are a few ideas we could do well to take advantage of.

● *Water* on the U.S. patio includes small mobile water features (Fig. 27) and shallow 'splash and paddle' pools used by adults as well as children in summer. Or a deep water 'hot tub', usually made of varnished timber, and large enough to take three or four adults sitting or standing. Sitting in warm water is just as pleasant in winter as in summer.

● *Sleeping out* is very common in more rural areas of the warmer States. The beds are often built-in and a particularly attractive idea is a wooden swinging bench between the timber uprights of a pergola which can be tilted and locked in place to form a 'hammock'.

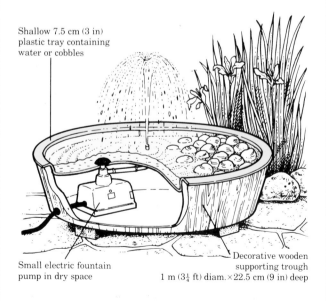

Shallow 7.5 cm (3 in) plastic tray containing water or cobbles

Small electric fountain pump in dry space

Decorative wooden supporting trough 1 m (3¼ ft) diam. × 22.5 cm (9 in) deep

Fig. 27 American-style portable pool.

● *Drop-down desks and tables* for working outdoors or playing board games – even sports like table tennis and darts (a folded table-tennis table is a mobile screen) – are a common feature and can be bought ready-made from garden shops and centres.

● *Garden stores.* Shade structures and timber uprights lend themselves to incorporating potting benches (Fig. 28) and work centres for general gardening or DIY. Mobile potting benches, with wheels and handles like a wheelbarrow, are also an idea worth stealing.

FURNISHING IDEAS

The first rule is not to buy any furniture until the patio is finished and planted to your satisfaction. Better to borrow anything you need from indoors than finish up with (from what nowadays is a very large choice) furniture that is too big, too small, or which does not blend in well with the overall picture. Chairs and tables can suddenly become a lot larger than they looked in the shop.

Up to a point, furniture should fit in with the style and materials of the house; although there are plenty of designs which can be folded and tucked away, and this is then not quite so important.

Think also of colour. Brightly painted furniture competes with the flowers, but looks good against foliage. White needs frequent washing. The pale green of *eau-de-nil* is an excellent choice which blends with everything. And, in this context, choose plain, rather than over-decorated fabrics for loungers, cushions, awnings and parasols. The garden itself must hold centre stage. Everything else must be just a well-picked collection of 'extras'.

Choosing the right furniture

It is very important to measure carefully when choosing chairs and tables for dining out. Remembering that the seating has to be drawn back when

·HANDY TIP·

Use mail order catalogues and send for manufacturers literature advertised in garden magazines to get a feel for what is available. This will save time and avoid a great deal of confusion.

people are sitting down or getting up, a space at least 2.5m (8ft) square must be allowed to take a table and four chairs. On a small patio, benching on two sides of a table, and chairs added on the free sides, saves space. If the space is sufficient for relaxation as well, then it is best to choose a table with folding leaves and folding or stacking chairs.

Lounging furniture should be comfortable, easy to use, and well balanced so that it does not tip up. Sunbeds with wheels save heavy lifting, but are expensive. Remember that plastic-coated fabrics stick to the skin in hot weather and fade quickly. Those with little space might consider a hammock between two posts, inflatable airbeds and plastic cushions, or beanbags.

● *Wooden furniture* is nearly always an all-year-round feature. For this purpose oak, elm or teak are best. Softwoods are cheaper but do not last so long and must frequently be painted or treated with preservative. Make sure wooden furniture is jointed, not just glued, and always rock it firmly to ensure it does not 'give'.

Metal fittings should be of non-corrosive steel or brass. And avoid polyurethane finishes which soon peel off outdoors.

Dress hardwood once a year with teak oil.

● *Metal furniture* should be top quality or it will rust and corrode when left outdoors and can also twist and distort on uneven surfaces. The heaviest is cast iron followed by cast aluminium, but these will take everything the weather can throw at

them if painted every year and any chips or signs of rust are properly repainted with primer and new paint.

As durable as solid metal is, it can be rather uncomfortable for prolonged sitting, although slim cushions help a little. Modern metal furniture, on the other hand, is comfortable and elegant and the designs coated with plastic do not need repainting.

● *Cane and rattan* are lightweight and attractive, although their lightness means they can be easily blown over. Taking them indoors is the answer as they will look equally good and especially suit the Victorian air of a conservatory – even a modern-style one. Paint them with clear gloss or satin polyurethane when they're new and never leave them out in the rain or cold, which encourages them to split and will eventually remove the varnish, encouraging rot.

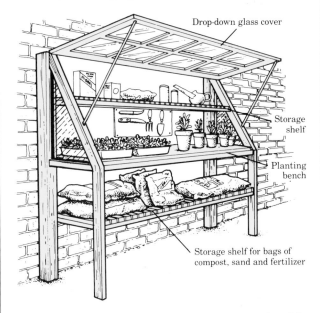

Fig. 28 **Wall-mounted potting bench – an unusual and useful idea from the States.**

87

◀ Built-in, solid hardwood seats add an attractive touch to this rustic brick patio.

▶ All-weather hardwood furniture and decking in a small town garden.

● *Synthetic resin, polycarbonate, or plastic furniture* is only now catching up with its potential and it may seem difficult to make a choice from the hundreds of brands. However, the vast majority have smooth, modern lines and are only available in white, so it is unlikely to prove such a problem and price will probably be the determining factor. When choosing, check backs and legs to ensure there are no moulding faults, or cracks which could snap when any real weight is put upon them. Make sure they are heavy enough to withstand wind and not be knocked over easily.

● *Second-hand furniture* is another alternative. Look around and use your imagination, too. Marble slabs can make wonderful tables, or even seats, with a substantial cushion. So can butcher's old wooden chopping boards. Cross-sections of tree-trunks supported on logs make attractive low coffee-tables. Old wooden furniture can be painted in matching colours. Old deckchairs or director-type chairs can be re-covered.

FOOD AL FRESCO

Although rather dependent on good weather, barbecues have become more popular as a family treat and especially as a social gathering, over recent years.

In its simplest form the barbecue is a charcoal fire with a grid over it on which sausages, chops and chicken pieces are cooked. At the other end of the scale, and on the larger patios, a built-in grill on mortared bricks, complete with a spit, griddle,

Fig. 29 Three types of ready-to-use barbecues.

(a) Gas (propane).

(b) Simple small charcoal burner.

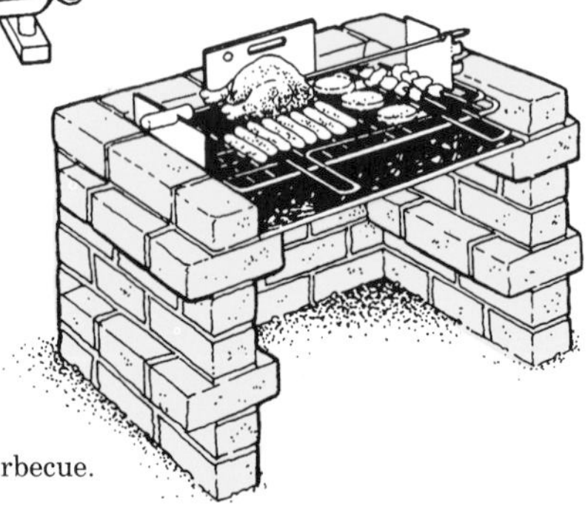

(c) Home-built brick barbecue.

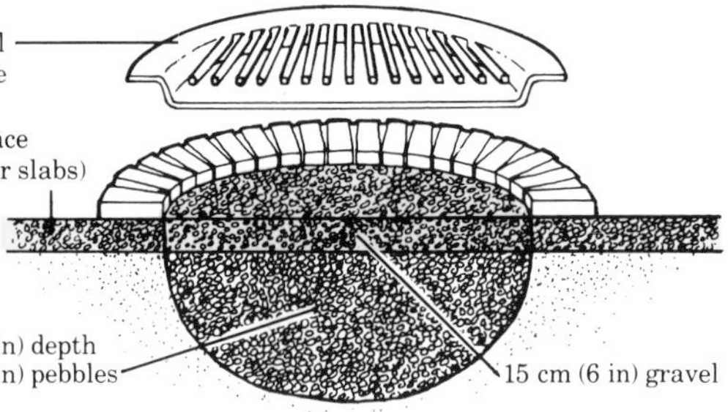

Safety grill and griddle

Patio surface (concrete or slabs)

50 cm (20 in) depth of 2 cm ($\frac{3}{4}$ in) pebbles

15 cm (6 in) gravel

Fig. 30 Construction of 'fire pit' barbecue.

charcoal burner, cinder catcher and shelves, set against a wall, is the ultimate luxury. Between these two extremes there are the simple metal-tray types, which are specially portable, and the more elaborate mobile barbecues in all sizes and types, some for traditional charcoal but many of them fuelled by gas or electricity.

Choosing a barbecue

The choice of barbecue depends upon space, how many people it has to serve ... and the size of your pocket! Most of the mobile ones have lockable wheels and some have useful working and serving surfaces (Fig. 29). Some also have hooks for tongs, spatulas, skewers, heat-proof gloves, and the bellows you may need if you are using charcoal. Some even come complete with these accessories. The most elaborate have motorized spits, rotisseries and hoods.

The metal parts of permanent and home-made barbecues must be removable for cleaning and for storing away when not in use. Portable and mobile ones must also be kept indoors between barbecues because most of them have some exposed metal parts that will rust if they are left standing out in all weathers.

● *Open fire* (Fig. 30). Lastly, the fire pit is an attractive barbecue style which is popular in the States. It is basically a hole in the ground over which the metal griddle is erected.

POOLS AND WATER

Ponds, nowadays, are a much simpler proposition as there are only two basic methods of construction – concrete and 'liners' – and on a patio a preformed, plastic or glass-fibre liner, or a flexible polythene, PVC or butyl one, is quite easy to install. Another type of small water feature is shown in Fig. 27 – an American style indoor/outdoor pool.

·HANDY TIP·

Half barrels make a novel water feature which can easily be moved and the design changed to suit tastes. But always line them with a pond liner material or heavy duty polythene because the wood can give out tanins which are poisonous to plants.

A pond or pool above ground level is safer for children or less able people and makes a slightly more unusual feature. When children are very small it can be filled with large cobbles with water bubbling over them. Similar alternatives could be water chuckling over a flat surface like a millstone, a stone or terracotta urn simply bubbling over, or half barrels planted with miniature water-lilies.

Practicalities

Keep ponds or pools away from trees and shrubs, which will fill them with rotting leaves. And water-lilies need six hours of sunshine a day, if possible, so the only really suitable place for water with anything alive in it, is out in the open.

Frogs and other small aquatic wildlife may move in but very small patio ponds are not really suited to fish as it is difficult to get the balance right for clear water.

Clear water

Still water needs the right plants, like water-lilies, and oxygenators such as Canadian pondweed, to keep the water clear. But don't expect it to clear right from the start – *all* pools turn green until the plants grow to cover at least three quarters of the surface and the water will then clear naturally and stay that way. So don't be tempted to clean it out or change the water.

Planting down

When it comes to selecting plants for a pool, it's always worth seeking out the help of a specialist nursery. Water-lilies and other submerged plants must be planted in special pots on the bottom of the pond, while 'water weeds' are simply weighted down.

If there is room for a shelf about 15cm (6in) under the water, plant 'marginals' such as water buttercup or marsh marigold, round the edges. These all need specialist plastic planters, too, in order that they can be removed easily and divided every few years as they become overcrowded.

·PLANTS FOR PONDS·

Name	Preferred site/Description
● IN WATER	
Japanese Iris (*Iris laevigata*)	Shallow water; blue iris flowers; three to a stem
Marsh marigold (*Caltha palustris*)	Shallow water; buttercup flowers; lush foliage
Monkey musk (*Mimulus luteus*)	Shallow water; yellow 'monkey face' flowers
Sweet flag (*Acorus calamus*)	Shallow water; striped leaves; white flowers in summer
Water hawthorn (*Aponogeton distachyus*)	Water 23–45 cm (9–18 in); floating leaves; cream/white divided flowers
Water lily (*Nymphaea × marliacea* 'Froebelli')	Water 30–75 cm (12–30 in); red, scented flowers; slow-growing
● IN WET OR BOGGY SOIL	
Astilbe (*Astilbe × arendsii*)	Feathery pink, mauve, red spikes; ferny, cut foliage
Candelabra primrose (*Primula pulverulenta*)	Tall floury stems; pink, orange, scarlet whorled flowers
Hostas (*Hosta sieboldii, H. fortunei*)	Blue, green, yellow, white, foliage; blue, white flowers
Houttuynia (*Houttuynia cordata* 'Chameleon')	Red, yellow, green foliage; creeping. White flowers
Water forget-me-not (*Myosotis palustris*)	Small, sky blue forget-me-not flowers

LIGHTING

Lighting can be temporary or permanent and, unless it requires a lot of cable, is more easily considered when the patio is completed.

As well as floodlights and spotlights, there are safety lights for steps, which are built into the risers, and low voltage lights using only 12 volts, the same as a car battery, working off a transformer hidden away safely in the dry somewhere. There are portable, battery-powered ones which are even safer. There are also very high-powered quartz iodide lights which make games and even gardening possible, in the dead of night!

Candle types range from bamboo poles fitted with flares that will burn for about two hours, to traditional but long-lasting wax ones which do not give so much light but will burn for days depending on size.

Most lights are provided with wall-fixtures, posts or spikes as appropriate, and many have additional attachments like interchangeable coloured filters or bulbs, directional hoods, and louvres to shade glare.

STATUES AND ORNAMENTS

Statues and ornaments are valuable additions but must be appropriate for the type of house and patio. A large reproduction Venus will look absurd in a small modern setting, whereas a bird bath or sundial looks attractive anywhere.

The smallest patio can still be decorated with wall-plaques and there are numerous examples of sober and amusing statuary – from bronze figures in modern dress and styles, to hedgehogs, old boots

◄ **Lights extend the flowering day and put the finishing touch to a summer evening in the garden.**

► **Graceful figures bring an air of peaceful serenity to secret corners of the garden.**

and the ubiquitous garden gnomes in real or reconstituted stone. But no statue or ornament, large or small, should be alone. They all appear more interesting against a wall, associated with plants and perhaps floodlit at night.

SAFETY AND SECURITY

Substantial construction will go a long way to providing peace of mind where safety is concerned, for example knowing that an arch, pergola, hanging basket, window box or trough is not going to collapse or fall on anyone.

Attention to general maintenance, repairs, painting, and cleaning, particularly moss and algae from steps, will also make the patio a much safer place. This assumes greater importance where it is adjoining the house and has to be used or crossed regularly during winter, even at night, when the effects of any shortcomings are magnified. Simply moving furniture out of the way or removing it completely at night or for storage, can prevent collision.

Covering the pond comes into this category too. Netting keeps out autumn leaves, but if it is tough wire netting on a wooden frame it could well prevent an unexpected, and potentially dangerous, accidental 'dip' as well.

Climbing ladders

When hanging baskets and window boxes need attention, or there are maintenance and cleaning jobs to do in higher places, always use a proper ladder. Preferably, if the height permits, a step ladder with a hand rail and top platform.

If an ordinary ladder has to be used, secure it firmly at the bottom or have someone hold it steady. Ladders should be kept at a tight angle to the wall. There is a danger of it sliding away if the bottom is too far out.

Electricity

Electricity is potentially more dangerous out of doors where it is more likely to come into contact with water. All electrical fittings and connections must be the heavy duty, outdoor, waterproof types and in good condition. A master circuit breaker covering all the outside equipment is advisable, too – this switches off the current automatically if there is a fault, or if a wire is accidentally damaged.

Disconnect any electrical equipment not in use in winter, including pond water pumps. Some lights are essential, though, and must be kept connected as they obviously prevent accidents. Lights set into the riser of steps and low, path-side lanterns are excellent for this.

Keeping one of the modern rechargeable torches plugged in and always to hand is a very good plan. They are extremely efficient and an invaluable safety aid on patios at night and in the winter.

Security

Security lighting systems are very sophisticated and can react to infrared heat given off by the body at several yards. They can be set to cover the patio area and it would then be reasonably safe to leave out garden furniture. But the simple security for other property is to lock the movable items away indoors or in a stout storage locker or shed.

High surrounding fences provide security as well as seclusion just by deterring would-be intruders. But this is a job which some shrubs are pretty efficient at, too. *Berberis julianae*, for instance, has long needle-like thorns and makes any attempt at forced entry through them very uncomfortable indeed.

A novel and harmless way to discourage 'peeping Toms' is to spread the tree-grease used for deterring fruit tree pests, along the top of high fences – but only if it is high enough to be out of reach and it will not affect or offend your neighbours!

Index

Page numbers in *italics* indicate an illustration or boxed table.

INDEX